The Tenderfoot In New Mexico

The Tenderfoot In New Mexico

Richard Baxter Townshend

New Foreword by
Marc Simmons

SOUTHWEST HERITAGE SERIES

SUNSTONE
PRESS

SANTA FE

Sunstone books may be purchased for educational, business, or sales promotional use.
For information please write: Special Markets Department, Sunstone Press,
P.O. Box 2321, Santa Fe, New Mexico 87504-2321.

Library of Congress Cataloging-in-Publication Data

Townshend, R. B. (Richard Baxter), 1846-1923.
  The tenderfoot in New Mexico / by Richard Baxter Townshend ; new foreword by
Marc Simmons.
     pages cm. -- (Southwest heritage series)
  Originally published: London : John Lane the Bodley Head, 1923.
  ISBN 978-0-86534-592-8 (softcover)
  1. New Mexico--Description and travel. 2. Townshend, R. B. (Richard Baxter),
1846-1923--Travel--New Mexico. 3. Ranch life--New Mexico--History--19th century.
4. British--New Mexico--Biography. I. Title.
  F801.T68 2013
  978.9'052092--dc23
  [B]
                                    2013029949

WWW.SUNSTONEPRESS.COM
SUNSTONE PRESS / POST OFFICE BOX 2321 / SANTA FE, NM 87504-2321 /USA
(505) 988-4418 / ORDERS ONLY (800) 243-5644 / FAX (505) 988-1025

CONTENTS

I

THE SOUTHWEST HERITAGE SERIES

"The past is not dead. In fact, it's not even past."
—William Faulkner, *Requiem for a Nun*

The history of the United States is written in hundreds of regional histories and literary works. Those letters, essays, memoirs, biographies and even collections of fiction are often first-hand accounts by people who wanted to memorialize an event, a person or simply record for posterity the concerns and issues of the times. Many of these accounts have been lost, destroyed or overlooked. Some are in private or public collections but deemed to be in too fragile condition to permit handling by contemporary readers and researchers.

However, now with the application of twenty-first century technology, nineteenth and twentieth century material can be reprinted and made accessible to the general public. These early writings are the DNA of our history and culture and are essential to understanding the present in terms of the past.

The Southwest Heritage Series is a form of literary preservation. Heritage by definition implies legacy and these early works are our legacy from those who have gone before us. To properly present and preserve that legacy, no changes in style or contents have been made. The material reprinted stands on its own as it first appeared. The point of view is that of the author and the era in which he or she lived. We would not expect photographs of people from the past to be re-imaged with modern clothes, hair styles and backgrounds. We should not, therefore, expect their ideas and personal philosophies to reflect our modern concepts.

Remember, reading their words and sharing their thoughts is a passport back into understanding how the past was shaped and how it influenced today's world.

Our hope is that new access to these older books will provide readers with a challenging and exciting experience.

II

FOREWORD TO THIS EDITION
by
Marc Simmons

Britishers were not uncommon on the American Southwestern frontier. Most of them, well-financed, came to acquire land and purchase cattle, intending to make their fortunes at ranching. But almost all were lured to America's Wild West as much by its romantic image as by the opportunity to grow rich.

One of the younger members of that breed of Englishmen was Richard Baxter Townshend, hungry for adventure and prosperity, who had only $100 in his wallet when he landed at the foot of the Colorado Rockies in 1869, just four years after the end of the Civil War. Townshend was then 23 years old and at that point had no experience in frontier living. Indeed, he was as green a tenderfoot as one could imagine. Born in 1846 into a well-off family classed as landed gentry, he attended a prestigious private school, then went on to Cambridge to take a degree at Trinity College. There, fellow students dubbed him "Cherub," because of his fair complexion, rosy cheeks, blue eyes, and curly hair.

Being a romantic sort with a streak of daring, young Townshend decided to immigrate to America's untamed West. Like Europeans then and now, he was captivated by cowboys and Indians. He would rub shoulders with innumerable examples of both during his years in Colorado and New Mexico.

For his first years, he remained footloose, roaming the country east of Colorado's Front Range and as far south as the Arkansas river. As he gained some seasoning and acquired a small block of capital, Townshend took a leap and bought a ranch on the plains 25 miles east of the future Colorado Springs. That drew him into the rough world of open-range cattle raising and hard-bitten cowboys.

By 1874, he was ready to try his hand at something new. Finding a buyer for the ranch who would pay it off in installments, Townshend with the first payment purchased a pair of freight wagons and two loads of dry goods, intending to drive to New Mexico and enter the Indian trade.

Once there, local merchants advised him to locate at Jemez pueblo west of the Rio Grande, where he would find a good demand for his wares. In addition, neighboring Navajos often came there to barter.

At Jemez, affable Townshend was welcomed like a long-lost brother. The Indians seemed to have liked his strange British accent. He described them as being "part of Montezuma's old empire," a popular fiction of the day.

The budding merchant in good time exchanged all his trade goods for pelts, raw wool, and Navajo blankets. These things he sold in Albuquerque for a large profit, allowing him to return to Colorado, his satchel stuffed with cash.

In 1877 Townshend received from his widowed mother in Wimbledon, England an urgent appeal to return home. He arrived there in mid-1877, having been absent for almost eight years. His own country had changed in the interval and he was uncomfortable in it, that is, until he met Letitia Jane Dorothea Baker, daughter of a clergyman.

Promptly, he became enamored of the lass, who was not only pretty but well-read in history and poetry. He would have proposed then and there, but lacked the money to begin married life. So hoping to earn "a quick stake," as he put it, he returned to Colorado with that in mind.

Renewing old friendships there, he learned that horses and mules were bringing large prices at the mining camp of Leadville. So he put together a trail crew and went to south Texas where those animals could be bought cheaply.

Putting together a large herd, Townshend and his men made a harrowing drive across Texas, and then ascended the Pecos river into New Mexico. On the way, they narrowly missed having the valuable livestock stolen by Billy the Kid and his outlaw pals.

Reaching Leadville at last, the animals were sold for a substantial profit. The extraordinary horse drive, with all its perils and hardships, is described in the final chapters of this book.

A few more profitable ventures and the sun-tanned Townshend returned to England at age 33, married Dorothea, and settled down to an altogether unadventurous life of writing, teaching, and playing lawn tennis.

He made one brief return to the Southwest in 1903, finding that the old Indians he had known were all dead and the cowboys, with the open range gone, were much tamed.

The last months of his life, Townshend spent pulling together his first book, *A Tenderfoot in Colorado*. It appeared from the press of an English publisher in February 1923. The following April 23 he died at Oxford in his 77th year.

The second volume, *The Tenderfoot in New Mexico*, was completed by devoted wife Dorothea, using notes left by her husband. It saw publication at the end of 1923. True to his memory, she collected a number of his magazine articles, mainly from the *Manchester Sunday Chronicle* together with his personal letters, all relating to Richard Townshend's final excursion to the Southwest, 1903–1904. These she combined to fill the pages of the final volume in the trilogy, *Last Memories of a Tenderfoot* (1926).

Of these, *The Tenderfoot in New Mexico* proved to be the most popular, with its descriptions of Townshend's experiences among the Pueblo and Navajo Indians, and his adventures on desert and mountain trails. Like the other two companion books, this one also contained much about western cattle ranching.

Although Townshend gained a wide audience in his day, among both Englishmen and Americans, by the mid 20th century he had slipped from public view. This new edition of *The Tenderfoot in New Mexico* by Sunstone Press will serve to re-introduce him to a new generation of readers.

III

EDITION OF 1923

THE TENDERFOOT IN
NEW MEXICO

R. B. TOWNSHEND
1882
From a drawing by Dorothea Townshend

THE TENDERFOOT
IN NEW MEXICO
BY R. B. TOWNSHEND

PREFACE

MAY I return thanks to the Editors of the periodicals in which some of the following reminiscences have appeared, for their kind permission to reprint?

The later chapters of this book have been arranged from notes written or dictated by my husband during the last weeks of his life. He died on the 28th of April, 1923, at Oxford, aged 77.

He was educated at Repton, and gained a minor scholarship at Trinity College, Cambridge, in 1865.

Soon after his death I received the following letter from the principal Chiefs of Jemez, the Indian pueblo described in this book:

"JEMEZ, NEW MEXICO,
                                    July 4.
"DEAR MRS. TOWNSHEND,

"Your letter of June 9, 1923, has reached us, and we sympathize with you. We had a meeting, and the old men of the Pueblo remember Mr. Townshend very well; the Indians thought very highly of him as Mr. Townshend was very kind to the Indians. We shall certainly remember the soul of Mr. Townshend in our prayers.

FRANCISCO MADULENA, *Gobernador*.
MARTIN SHENDOH, *Assistant*.
JOSE ROMERO, *Principale*."

The photographs of Jemez reproduced in the following pages were taken by my husband in 1903, in Jemez. On his drive up the Pecos he had no time to think of making pictures.

DOROTHEA TOWNSHEND.

CONTENTS

LIST OF ILLUSTRATIONS

THE TENDERFOOT IN
NEW MEXICO

CHAPTER I

ADIOS, COLORADO

I HAVE already told in my book, *A Tender-foot in Colorado*, how I went out to the Far West in 1869, and after some five years of travel and cattle-ranching in Colorado I sold out my ranch and stock there and decided to try New Mexico. I had now for partners two men of Spanish blood from Old Mexico who had been working for me as herders. Both the men spoke English well and could read and write, which very few New Mexicans could do. The older, Leonardo Garcia, generally known as " Gus," had been a cowboy for many years in Texas and Colorado ; the other man, Vicente Elias, was much younger than Gus ; also he was a bit of a dare-devil. He had fought under Porfirio Diaz and helped in the overthrow of the ill-fated Emperor Maximilian. I can recall still his shout of " Viva Porfirio Diaz " when we talked of that struggle.

Both men had saved a little money, and we

three purchased a couple of wagon-loads of goods which we proposed to take down to New Mexico and trade off there. That fearlessness of his was the point in Vicente's character which particularly attracted me. I remember well a certain trip which he made with me down to the Spanish Peaks. This was just before I had parted with my ranch, and I had got an idea of finding a new place to take up in Southern Colorado. I had heard of a certain Lost Park down on the Picket-wire, and I hoped there I should find it less crowded.

So leaving Gus to look after the ranch, Vicente and I saddled our horses and started off down to the Spanish Peaks. All the arms I had along consisted of one butcher's knife. It is true that I had some reason for what I did. Just then there were no hostile Indians in that part of Colorado. Also I wanted to leave my pistol with Gus, who was to stay behind and take care of the ranch. Also I wouldn't have a rifle with me, because I didn't want to be tempted to waste my time in hunting, seeing that I was after a new cattle ranch.

It was late summer when we started, and we got down to the Picket-wire country all right. But no " Lost Park " could we find.

" Look here, Vicente," said I, " I'll tell you what we'll do. Let's climb the highest of those two Spanish Peaks. We'll get a bird's-eye view of all creation from on top. If that Lost Park's anywhere round here it's bound to be visible from up there."

Now, as it happened, by this time our souls lusted after fresh meat. Bacon and flour had been the supplies with which I loaded our pack-horse for the trip; we had been out a fortnight, and hot bread and fat bacon for breakfast, dinner and supper had palled on us long since. So we ate but a few morsels at a meal, and even so our supplies were running short. Deer we saw often; of course as we had no gun, they would stand a good minute or more within fifty yards of us as we rode by, to tantalize us, it's a little way they have. But, to our joy, on the lower slopes of the Spanish Peaks we encountered a travelling Mexican sheep herd. Vicente knew how to deal with the man in charge of a Mexican sheep herd to a T. " Carne por dinero," he cried to the swarthy peon who shepherded the flock, " carne por dinero." And the offer of " cash for meat " fetched him. He captured and killed a fat young goat out of his flock. A dollar was transferred from my pocket to his, and the whole of that carcass, with its tempting kidney fat, was tied on top of our pack. Hurrah! No more greasy bacon for us; no more indigestible hot bread; no getting up hungry from a loathed dinner. Savoury meat we would have, such as our souls loved.

Up and up we climbed, and camped for the night at the upper edge of the timber where there was pretty good grass for the horses. We hobbled them out and collected quantities of dry wood for our fire. It was cold up here on the heights, and then, besides, there was that goat to cook. We made long spits of wood and skewered thereon and broiled over the coals sweet slices of the tender meat. Oh, how sweet it tasted !

But as we sat by the glowing embers in the intense starlight of the sierra there burst upon the air a sudden, wild, unearthly scream quite close to us. " Los leones," cried Vicente, jumping up. " That the cry of the mountain lions. I wonder if they stampede them horses."

We listened and we heard the hobbled horses plunging about. " Come on," said Vicente, and we ran towards them, shouting to scare the lions and calling the horses in horse language to assure them that it was all right. Nothing calms a terrified horse so much as the voice of a man he knows. We found our animals scared and trembling, and patted them till they partially recovered their courage. Then we led them right into our camp, and piled on chunks of fat pine to make a blaze and the terrified creatures rejoiced in its protecting light.

" I guess them lions don't bother us long," said Vicente as we listened intently for the cry of the wild beasts. " They don't attack big horses now at this time of year ; young colts are what they go for if deer get scarce ; in winter, if they mighty hungry, maybe they try to kill big horse, but in summer I think they rather hunt deer. Deer meat mighty good."

So said Vicente, drawing the spit with the ribs off the ground. They were roasted to a turn and were as delicious as venison. All of a sudden he sprang to his feet. " I guess these lions like the smell of our meat," he said, and he flung a rock at something very near us in the darkness outside the ring of light. " Go off," he shouted. " You lion, go away. Leave us alone, and go hunt deer."

And presently he was answered from across the gully by a prolonged and bitter wail, this time an undoubted scream of disappointment.

" Bless these confounded lions ! " said I. " I want to go to bed. But I don't seem to care about these guardian angels."

" Mean devils, I call them," said Vicente. " Best thing we do is sit up and keep fire going so these horses don't get stampeded."

It was very annoying, certainly. But then we had the goat to console us. And so Vicente and I sat up and told stories, and broiled and ate succulent goat meat the livelong night.

When morning dawned at last the horses were all right, and so were we ; but the lions and the goat had vanished. The lions had at last concluded that they had better sup elsewhere, and as for the goat it had vanished down our throats. Our excuse must be that we were both of us young and hearty, we had half-starved ourselves for over a week, and we were most desperately hungry for fresh meat.

Next day Vicente and I left the horses to graze about timber-line while we climbed to the very highest point of the Spanish peaks. North and south we beheld the mighty wall of the Rocky Mountains stretching for three hundred miles, with the Great Plains rolling like a boundless ocean against their base.

Then downwards we plunged again on our way back to the spot where we had left our camp and our horses. Vicente was ahead, having out-stripped me a little, and we were already off the rocks, and on the edge of the open grassy land, when I heard him shout excitedly, and I had a glimpse of him dashing forward in chase of two little reddish-yellow furry creatures that fled before him. He and his quarry were out of my sight in a moment, but I set off running too, and presently round the corner of a huge rock I came into full view. It was a case of gone to ground. All that was visible of Vicente were his legs wriggling wildly in the air, while his body and head had disappeared in the depths of a hole at the foot of the rock.

" What is it ? " I panted eagerly as I came up.

" Little lions," came back the answer in a half-stifled voice from the interior of the den, " two little lions, quite small."

By a desperate struggle he seemed to worm himself about a foot farther in. Then I heard him exclaim in disappointed tones, " No puedo. I can't reach them."

My eyes were busy scanning the rocks all round.

" Hurry up, man," cried I. " Suppose the old ones come back and catch us ! These mountain lions aren't anything to fool with. You've no weapon at all, and I've got nothing but a butcher-knife."

An angry mountain lion is no despicable foe ; didn't a single Florida panther (which is the same creature under another name) kill one Englishman and mortally wound another in about half a minute in defence of her young ? And those men had guns.

But Vicente was a dare-devil. He only redoubled his efforts, though he thought I said that the lions were coming, actually coming.

" Heave rocks at them," he gasped, still struggling to get at the cubs. " Heave big rocks. Break their heads."

This was a truly Homeric style of combat, to which I hardly felt equal ; happily the lions were not in sight, neither did they appear on the scene, charging to the rescue, before Vicente, hot, breathless, and marked with abundant stains of mother earth, emerged at last into the light of day. But he came out empty-handed.

" Where are the cubs ? " I asked.

" Too far in," he panted, making an attempt to get rid of some of the soil that clung to his clothes and hair. " That hole got too small for me inside."

" Well, come along," said I impatiently. " You can titivate yourself in camp. All the time that you were grubbing away down in there, I've been expecting to be bounced by a pair of infuriated parents regularly foaming at the mouth. But you hear me talk, my name isn't Daniel, and I'm not camping in lions' dens not for choice this journey. I've not lost any lion cubs."

" They got up right under my feet," said Vicente regretfully, looking back. " I could have lassoed one of them if I'd had my rope with me. I did so want a little lion for a pet." And with lingering steps he followed me as I led the way back to camp.

The horses seemed to have been feeding peacefully. There was no sign of any lions having been near them, and we were soon in the saddle once more and riding downward through the forests. But we were not destined to leave the Spanish Peaks without a peep at the lions after all. I was in front, with Vicente just behind leading the pack-horse. Suddenly, right in the trail before me, I caught sight of a tawny creature as big as a calf. I reined up short.

" The lions ! The lions, Vicente ! " I exclaimed.

" Laze-lo ! laze-lo ! " he cried in great excitement. " Lasso him, lasso him ! "

" Great Scott ! " said I. " Not much I don't ! "

" Well, hold the pack-horse then," he cried,

spurring up alongside me and passing me the halter. His hands trembled with eagerness as he began to untie the rope he had on his saddle.

But the lion had no mind to be lassoed. For one moment he looked at us, then he swiftly bounded to one side, and stretched away through the trees like a tawny streak. Pursuit was hopeless.

" But, Vicente," said I, as he was coiling his rope while we moved forward again, " what could you possibly have done if you had lassoed him ? You couldn't throw him and tie him as you might a cow."

" Maybe yes, if you bin able to help me," said he. " By myself, perhaps no."

That was Vicente all over.

This adventure reminds me of another occasion while I was at the ranch, when I ought to have had a gun, and hadn't. Though a little belated, I may set it down here.

I was coming back one time from a buffalo hunt with a heavy wagon-load of meat and hides. The rest of the party were in another wagon, and as theirs was a spring wagon I carelessly left my trusty Sharpe's rifle to be carried in it to save jolting. We had calculated to make the big waterhole on Horse Creek that evening ; but it was winter and the days were short, and the shades of night began to fall before we had quite reached it.

" I'll just trot on," called out Claude Duval,

the driver of the other wagon, turning round to me, "and you can follow our tracks. We'll get a fire started and have supper ready for you."

So they went ahead, he and I both thinking that Horse Creek was now only a mile or two distant. Duly I followed their tracks one mile, two miles, three miles; but no signs of Horse Creek appeared; no welcome fire; no supper. The distance had been miscalculated. Then it grew to be black night, and I could no longer follow their tracks; I began to be rather uneasy; here I was out on the Great Plains, alone and unarmed. This thing happened in the days before the country was settled, while the buffalo and the wild Indian still reigned the monarchs of the prairie.

Well, there was nothing for it but to push on. If I steered west by the stars I was bound to hit Horse Creek before morning. So I pushed on, and somewhere towards midnight I did hit it; alas, there was no light of any friendly fire visible, no waterhole, no camp! Were my companions farther up the Creek, or farther down? That was what I wanted to know. If I drove north and their camp lay to the south I should only be going away from them, and vice versa. That didn't seem good enough, and I decided to stop right where I was. Luckily in the sandy bed of Horse Creek I stumbled upon an old buffalo camp where there was any quantity of dry buffalo chips, so that I needn't freeze, although not only my rifle but my blankets were in the other wagon. I picketed out my two mules, spread a green buffalo hide over the wheels to make me a wind-break, started a good fire of chips, and set to work toasting bits of buffalo beef, for I was hungry as well as tired out. To eat seemed the only thing to do, for it was too cold to sleep.

And then, some time after midnight, came a long drawn " Ow-ow-ow-w-w." It was the howl of a big grey wolf; he had smelt the meat and wanted some of it for himself, wanted it bad. The terrified mules snorted loudly and ran round their pickets, till I got up and brought them into the ring of light by the fire. The howl came nearer; it came quite close; a form was darkly seen on the outskirts of the ring; the wolf was there. I shouted at him, but he declined to go. I threw a buffalo chip at him. He shifted a bit, sat down on his tail, and howled longer than ever. It was a gruesome sound; he was calling to his companions to come to supper. " Meat," he was calling to them, " fresh me-e-at."

And me? Well, I was not happy. I was swearing at myself for having played tenderfoot, for allowing myself to be parted—ever—from my well-beloved rifle out on the plains. And I was thinking what to do if that long howl was answered and the whole wolf pack arrived. I threw more chips on the fire and threw some more also at the dark form that hovered round the edge of the light. The big grey wolf shifted again, and he howled again till the mules sweated with fear. The smell of that wagon-load of raw meat so close to him must have been maddening.

My plan, the only plan I could think of, if those whom he was calling did come, was to cut the mules loose, jump on one, and skip in any direction I could through the darkness. Perhaps the wolves would be satisfied with plundering the wagon. Perhaps—and I listened for the answering howl.

But the great buffalo herd where we had been shooting was thirty or forty miles off farther east, and the army of wolves hung ever upon its flanks ; that was where all the best pickings were to be had. My friend on the edge of the ring was playing a lone hand just then—who knows why ?— and his call was not answered. Slowly the hours drew towards dawn. By turns I made up the fire and pelted him with chips till the east grew grey ; then I put the harness on my team, and when daylight came I hitched them up and rolled out in the direction where I saw the smoke of the camp. My friend of the night followed me still at a little distance ; the smell of the raw meat in the wagon drew him like a tow-rope, but when we came near and he spotted several men moving around he quickly scented danger and cleared off before I had time to get my Sharpe's rifle and turn the tables on him.

It was after our return from the Spanish Peaks that Vicente and I and Gus started on the trail to New Mexico. Gus drove one wagon and Vicente the other, and the first place we were to make for was the Rio Cucharas in Southern Colorado, where lived a certain Don Elias de la Rosa on a small ranch. He was an old friend of Gus and Vicente and, like them, he hailed from Old Mexico.

Don Elias, however, was a family man ; he had married a lady from New Mexico, and now, having got tired of Colorado, he had disposed of his ranch and was minded to go back to New Mexico again. So he joined our party with a third wagon which carried his wife and six children, the eldest of whom, a girl named Manuelita, was engaged to marry Vicente.

It was a rough and long journey of some two hundred miles, for our road led us over the mountains into the San Luis Park and thence in a line roughly parallel to the upper Rio Grande down to the lower part of that river where the older Mexican settlements were. It was an uneventful journey, though¹ slow, for our wagons were heavily loaded. Myself, I rode my favourite mount Black Tom, who was not of ordinary bronco stock but a Kentucky horse, nearly thoroughbred, which I had bought some time before. For arms I had along a 16-shot Winchester, taking the old ·44 rimfire copper cartridge, as well as an up-to-date ·45 Colt's pistol. The mountain Indians were peaceful just then, unlike their red brethren of the Great Plains, but with Indians you never can tell, and in an unsettled country it is always best to go well heeled.

I knew practically no Spanish at this time, yet here I was off to a country where 25 per cent of the people spoke nothing else and, perhaps, not one in a hundred could read and write. So I thought I had better learn Spanish as quick as ever I could and I picked up a good deal from Don Elias' family. Black Tom was as tame as a dog, so I could turn him loose to travel with the wagons, picking up a bit of grass as he went along, while I myself walked up the hills (which were many) with the delightful children and picked up Spanish. The Señora de la Rosa, the mother, was a daughter of Don Tomas Cabeza de Vaca, the head of one of the greatest families in New Mexico. That country, which is not much smaller than France, had become a Territory of the United States, being part of the large slice which the Americans carved off from Old Mexico after the war of 1846. It was not a slave country, because Mexico had abolished slavery after she got clear of Spain, but the poor people, the Mexican peons, stood in almost as much awe of the great landowners as do slaves of their masters. Things have changed now in this twentieth century; American settlers have poured in and, I am told, constitute an actual majority, but at the time of which I speak I doubt if they were 5 per cent of the population.

Glad I was that I had learned some Spanish,

when our long journey ended at Peña Blanca on the lower Rio Grande, where Don Tomas lived and where Gus and I saw Vicente happily married to the Señorita Manuelita de la Rosa, granddaughter of Tomas Cabeza de Vaca.

The name means "Head of a Cow," an old name even in Spain; and it was originally given by a king of Spain to a shepherd boy who helped him at a very opportune moment by showing him a trail up the mountain at Tolosa, so that he could successfully attack the Moorish enemy. To mark the trail the boy was clever enough to stick up into a tree the head of a cow killed by wolves. The king found the trail, took the fort, and gave the useful boy the romantic title of Cabeza de Vaca.

One of the family, Alvar Nunez Cabeza de Vaca, was among the most famous of the Spanish conquistadores of the New World, and it is recorded of him that, unlike some conquerors, he ruled his Indian subjects with justice and mercy. His traditions were carried on by his descendants. I was amused to notice the awe with which the peons spoke of the head of the house, and by this time I had learned enough Spanish to ask an old man who had served the Vacas for some seventy years, why he held Don Tomas in such reverence. He answered simply : "Quizas poco atras de Dios Don Tomas." "Perhaps Don Tomas is a little less than God Almighty," I was answered.

CHAPTER II

AFTER no long stay at Peña Blanca we fixed on a place called Jemez as a good centre for us to start our trading. It was some thirty miles west of Peña Blanca on a small river that ran into the Rio Grande a bit lower down. We chose it because it was almost the farthest west of any of the Mexican settlements and the Navajos used to come in there to trade off their sheepskins and the beautiful ɔlankets that their squaws wove from the wool of their flocks.

The Navajos were a very fine tribe of redmen who were regular nomads; New Mexico was nine-tenths of it wilderness, and they wandered over all the north-west portion of it. A truly industrious and go-ahead tribe they were, for they raised many thousands of sheep and grew patches of corn in spots where the ground was damp enough, and also they bred horses. Because they were so industrious, of course they were properly despised by the Colorado Utes, who thought of nothing and cared for nothing but hunting and taking other men's scalps. But,

NAVAJO PEDDLING FRUIT

when it came to fighting, the Navajo braves, if
not quite such warriors as the Utes, were no
slouches at that either, as the United States had
found a few years before when they tackled
them. But when it came to war with the white
man, discipline and repeating rifles proved too
much for Indian valour. The Navajos were
beaten and surrendered. To teach them a lesson
the United States moved them over to the Pecos
on the east side of New Mexico and kept them
there under guard. Naturally they died off like
flies—savages under guard are apt to do so—and
the heart-rending wails that went up from the
prisoners there on the Pecos make one think of
Israel in Egypt. But the heart of the American
Government was not hardened as was Pharaoh's
heart; and they settled to let the people go.
Joyful indeed were the Navajos to get back to
their own dear land. They had promised to be
good boys in future if they might return, and they
kept their promise, except in the little matter of
stealing Mexican sheep and horses to make a
fresh start as pastoralists. But they did really
and truly stop killing people, at which they used
to be adepts, and they liked killing shepherds
especially. The great Mexican families had huge
herds of sheep, which travelled in flocks of one
or two thousand each, guarded by two or three
Mexican peons, who had been bred as shepherds,
all over the great uninhabited ranges up to the
edge of the Navajo country. There was lots of

c

room for them : let me say it again.   New Mexico is nearly as big as France, and now that the Navajos were on their good behaviour the shepherds were safe even if a few of the sheep were missing.

Also, as I said, these Indians did love horses. They used them for riding and racing, not for work, for naturally they did not have anything so civilized as carts or ploughs, and they used them also for eating.   They just loved horseflesh. So if a Navajo was disappointed in his horse as a racer he simply let him grow fat and then butchered him and made a grand feast for all his friends and relations.   Possibly this helped to improve the breed of horses.   Anyhow they had some very good ones.   One result of this Navajo weakness for good horses was that when we were trading at Jemez I parted with Black Tom lest he should be stolen, and I sold him to an Englishman who had come down to Santa Fé to try his luck as a doctor.   Then I bought a California mare of the ordinary bronco stock of the country to ride instead.

But beside the Navajos there was another lot of Indians who came to trade with us, and they did not have far to come, for they lived right there.   These were the Indians of the Pueblo de Jemez, a little lower down the river than the Mexican village.   Unlike the wandering Navajos they lived in houses, and their pueblo, or village, formed a sort of fort in which they had in the

JEMEZ WOMEN GRINDING CORN WITH METATE, WHILE A MAN AMUSES
THEM BY BEATING A DRUM

remote past defended themselves successfully against Navajos and Apaches and other hostile tribes. I believe they were part of Montezuma's old empire, but they accepted Spanish over-lordship after the conquest and became nominal Christians. The Spaniards let them keep their pueblos and also granted them their lands. Accordingly they went on living in their homes, being about the most peaceful and industrious people in the whole country. At this time they possessed a good herd of horses, guarded by their young men up in the sierra, and these were brought down when wanted; and they also owned a herd of cattle. They milked their cows and broke their steers to work and used them for hauling their ploughs and drawing their carts, an art which I suppose they learned from the Spaniards who first brought them into contact with domestic animals. Their wolfish dogs, no doubt, like those of other Indian tribes, had already been domesticated before ever the white men came to America.

Talking of dogs, I should like to tell a little thing that happened to me in Santa Fé with regard to them. I had ridden in from Jemez on my mare, and following me I had a Mexican, who drove one of our wagons laden with sheep-skins and pelts and blankets, for which we had traded both with Mexicans and Indians. I put up my mare at the El Paso corral, and mindful of the law against firearms being carried in town

I left my Colt's pistol at the hotel where I was going to stop. Then I sallied forth to call on my good friends, Mr. Johnson, and the Spiegelberg brothers, and others who kept big stores in Santa Fé, where they bought just such stuff as I had brought along and sold flour and coffee and bacon and lots of other necessary goods. I found out what prices they were asking for their stuff and what they were prepared to give for mine, and then I went on to a very enterprising Jew, Solomon Stendhal, whom I had dealt with previously and rather liked for himself as well as his prices. I rather liked his prices this time too, and our talk led to his proposing to take me out into the corral behind his store to show me some extra good bacon he was sure I should appreciate. A Jew Solomon might be, but that didn't prevent his dealing in hog products such as bacon or in his being an uncommon good judge of the quality of it, either.

Solomon produced his keys, unlocked the door, and we stepped into the corral. As I did so two huge Cuban bull-mastiffs sprang to the very end of their chains gnashing their great teeth with fury and making as though they would like to tear me limb from limb. Solomon looked at the brutes with an admiring grin.

"Ah, dem's de boys," he said enthusiastically as he faced square round at me. "Dem's de real man-eaters. I turns 'em loose in here every night and you bets your boots no dam

rascal thief, no Mexican, no nigger, no Indian
ever steal one thing. If he come in here
dem dogs eats him, eats him raw without
salt."

"Yes, they're fine dogs all right," said I.
"But what's to prevent the thief from having
his gun along, and then where would your dogs
be?"

"Ah," scoffed Solomon, "dem dogs too quick
for him. Dey eats him just the same. No
man's gun stop 'em."

"Well," returned I, "the law forbids the
carrying of firearms here in town and I haven't
got my pistol on. But you let me go back to
the corral and fetch my army Colt here and you
can turn your dogs loose and I'll bet you a hundred
dollars they don't eat me."

The Jew's eyes fairly glowed, for he was as
keen as mustard on a sporting game. Down
went his hand into his pocket. I had just been
to the bank myself and down went my hand into
my pocket for my full wallet, and I brought
out a hundred-dollar note which I held out on
my outstretched palm.

"Cover that," said I, "and it's a match."

The Jew carefully counted out a hundred
dollars in smaller notes and raised his hand with
the bundle of notes in it as if to cover my stake.
Then he lowered his hand again and shoved the
notes back into his pocket.

"No," he said, "I don't lose one real good

customer like you for no hundred dollars—but dem dogs eats you all de same."

After which, of course, I could not but buy the supplies we wanted from Solomon.

CHAPTER III

AN INDIAN PUEBLO

THE two principal white men at this time in the Jemez valley were living, not among the Mexicans, but in the Pueblo de Jemez among the Indians. One of them, John Miller, had a small post under the U.S. Indian Department in the pueblo ; the other, Judge Beaumont, was an old Californian pioneer who had come to New Mexico to prospect, for though by profession he was a lawyer, in practice he was a miner. He had joined with John—who was also a keen prospector—in more than one search for gold out in the mountains towards the Navajo country, but, search as they might, their luck only allowed them merely to find " the colour " which does not take you very far, for it does not necessarily mean " pay gravel," which is what's wanted. So they had chucked prospecting and returned to the pueblo, where John had three good rooms rented and where the pair did their own cooking and fended for themselves. Squaw men, as men who live with Indian women are called, they were not.

I liked very much to listen to the Judge's

California yarns of the old times, but he did not stay much longer at Jemez : he went over to San Isidro, a Mexican village on the Rio Grande, and established himself there looking after the interests of a California company in some land grant. John, of course, stayed on at Jemez, and he and I became great friends.

It was quite odd the way John came to be there. He was of a Pennsylvania family—I'm not sure if they weren't Quakers originally—and his elder brother had been appointed Indian Agent for the Navajos out at Fort Defiance just across the New Mexico line in Arizona. This was after the war with the Navajos, which ended in their being taken as captives over to Bosque Redondo and finally restored to their own country. Mr. Miller senior, now having the job of managing them, got out his brother John to help him as an employé of the Department, and John, always a keen rifle shot, soon became a fine frontiersman. Then a most unhappy thing happened. Certain Navajos—not the tribe, John was clear about that—got a down on Mr. Miller, and while he was travelling round on the reservation these enemies of his treacherously crept into his camp on the San Juan one night, and there murdered him and his companion while they slept. John always upheld that this was a private piece of spite, and he never blamed the Navajo nation for it, but the actual murderers only. These were never punished—no conclusive evidence could be got—

but, of course, there had to be a new Agent at Defiance, and John, partly perhaps as a sort of compensation, was given a small departmental post on his own in Jemez Pueblo ; this was what had brought him there.

He was a splendid shot, and we often went together up into the sierra after deer and turkey, which were plentiful there. Naturally, I enjoyed my life in New Mexico very much. But it was destined to a most tragic interruption.

Vicente Elias most rashly allowed himself to be drawn to take sides in certain local political factions, which were very bitter. Of course, he was no novice : he had played the game of politics before in Old Mexico : I could well remember his enthusiastic shout of " Viva Porfirio Diaz ! " in honour of the liberator of his country from Maximilian. In Old Mexico, however, life was cheap and politics and murder went hand-in-hand, as Vicente well knew. New Mexico ought to be quite different, for here we were, nominally at least, under the more civilized rule of the United States, and it did seem as if things ought to be much better. Alas! they proved to be as bad, if not worse, and one night, when Garcia and I were both of us absent and were known by the hostile party to be absent, poor Vicente was shot dead through a window. The actual murderers were not discovered, though we could make a pretty good guess at them, and guessed too that they would expect Gus and me to try to revenge our friend on them. We two were therefore in serious danger. We decided it would be wisest to dispose of our stock-in-trade and pay the poor young widow her share, and then for Gus at least to leave that part of the country.

I was unwilling to bolt back to Colorado. The money to be paid there for my ranch and stock was not yet due—and also the stories of fortunes to be made by prospecting which I had heard from Mexicans, as well as from the Judge and John Miller, had fired my ambition to start on the search for gold. But, most important of all, I was deeply anxious to get justice done on the murderers and I could not be content to fly to safety and let the matter drop. The great Don Tomas was now too old to stir in the matter, so I went over to Bernalillo and had an interview there with Don Francisco P., a Mexican grandee, who was the leading man of the side to which Vicente had joined himself. Of course, he knew all about the affair, as well as about me.

" Esperate, wait," said he, when I gave him the names of the suspected murderers and asked what could be done to secure their punishment. " Wait, have patience ! Their side is in now, and it is perfectly useless to bring them before any of the courts. The murderers of that side are protected by their bosses. But our time will come ! Some day we shall win the elections and we shall be back in power again ; and then, oh, but they shall suffer for their sins ! "

Don Francisco was an elderly man, obviously very astute, and he knew his country. There was nothing for it but to wait. But where was that to be done ? Naturally I felt a good deal on my nerves going about among the Mexicans.

Then John Miller solved the difficulty. He was feeling a bit lonely now that the Judge had left him and he suggested that I should come and share his rooms in the Indian pueblo.

" You'll be all right if once you come and hitch up with me," said John. " The Jemez Indians haven't much use for Mexicans except at a distance. They own their land by grant from Government ; they've got four square leagues with the pueblo in the centre ; and you bet they're mighty careful to keep the Mexicans off of it, and they see just as little of them as they can ; you bet your boots the Jemez bucks watch 'em mighty close if any of 'em do come around. You see the Jemez people are pure blood Indian ; they won't never let any Mexican get any chance at their women ; it's a point of honour with them ; there are some pueblos where they've mixed the breed, but not here, and Jemez is proud of it, mighty proud. It don't make any odds to them that a Catholic priest, a Mexican, comes over from Bernalillo every few months and gives them a service in the church. They call themselves Catholics, but I reckon there's a good deal of their old religion attended to on the quiet. But I don't ask no questions, and the

Jemez 'folk like Americans so long as they let their women alone, and they've heard all about you and the kind of man you are. You just come along and live with me and they'll be more than pleased."

Willingly I closed with his offer and took up my quarters at Jemez. Soon I got to like the Indians very much. Of course, I talked with them in Spanish, of which they had good working knowledge ; I am sorry now that I did not try to learn their own Jemez tongue, which they always used among themselves

The pueblo was built of adobe, that is to say, of mud-bricks dried in the sun. A few of the living-houses were separate, but most were in blocks one, two, or three stories high with flat mud roofs. The roofs were made by laying long poles eight inches or so in diameter, some three feet apart, across from wall to wall ; on the poles were laid smaller sticks close together, and on these was plastered thick the red clay of the country which resisted water well. I never remember any rain getting through on to us. Oddly enough the houses belonged not to the men of the pueblo but to the women : we rented our flat, if I may call it so, not from Victoriano, the master of the house, but from his squaw Reys. They were a fine young couple in the prime of life with some beautiful children, whom they carefully kept from getting into our way.

There was another thing, too, which perhaps

PUEBLO DE JEMEZ

helped to keep our quarters clear of too many visitors, and that was Keno. Keno was John's brindled bulldog. He had been reared in Santa Fé as a fighting dog, but John had got hold of him through a friend and brought him out to the pueblo where he made him his beloved bedfellow and taught him to hunt deer or anything else that might turn up. Keno, having been raised among the Mexicans of Santa Fé, did not love Indians, but he was devoted to John and obeyed him so far as not to go for them unnecessarily. But we kept an eye on him when we had visitors, which was pretty often, for John was popular.

Small wonder, too, if he was so. The Jemez people had no end of glorious peach orchards and ploughlands which they cultivated either with clumsy wooden ploughs drawn by oxen or with huge hoes, and these lands were watered from an acequia madre or main ditch drawn from the Jemez river quite a long way up. This acequia had to be carried round a point of rocks rising above the river in one place, and here it was always breaking down. John, who was a practical miner, saw what was wanted, put in a few blasts of powder, and blew out a lot of the obnoxious rock, so that the Indians could run their ditch twice as full round the point and never have it break down. He halved their labour and increased their crops of corn immensely, and every single man and woman in the pueblo felt personally grateful to him.

Even though I had not wrought any such crowning mercy on their behalf I soon became the best of friends with them : so thoroughly did they adopt me that they gave me an Indian name of my own, Poshiyemo, which was the name of their dawn god, in honour of my rosy cheeks and blue eyes.

Here let me anticipate and relate a curious experience that I had in connection with that name nearly thirty years after, when I paid a flying visit to New Mexico and stayed with John Miller and his American wife in a charming house he had built up in the mountains near Jemez Hot Springs.

John and I drove down to the pueblo on the day of one of their important fiestas, and long before we got there we heard the call of the Indian drums, a curiously wild and exciting sound. The young braves of the tribe, men from seventeen to thirty, were galloping wildly about on their ponies. Each had his long hair tied up at the back in a thick club bound with braid, while the sidelocks were kept from blowing into his face by a red handkerchief twisted round his brows. Their gaudy-coloured shirts were gathered round the waist by a cartridge belt and the skirts fluttered free below, for the Indian wears his shirt outside his leggings.

I picked out a good group, raised my camera and loosed off at them. In an instant they all closed round me, very much excited and not over

JOHN MILLER AT HOME

friendly. It was curious to see the dark faces and dark eyes so eagerly bent on me, while they demanded what right I had to make pictures there without leave or payment.

"Nada," said I, smiling, "you don't expect me to pay like a tourist; I am at home here."

"Who are you?" they cried. "What's your name?"

"Poshiyemo," said I. "Poshiyemo was my name when I was here before, and that was before any of you were born." There was a great shout of laughter from the ring. They crowded on me till their horses' noses were almost up against the camera.

"The Poshiyemo!" they cried with more bursts of laughter.

"Why certainly," I said. "Go and ask the old men?"

Some of the young braves took me at my word and galloped off. In a very few minutes they were back waving their hands amicably.

"It's all right; he's a friend, he can do as he likes," and they dispersed again to their games.

I made my pictures in peace, and looked up the few of my old Indian friends who still survived.

But that was thirty years on.

At the time that I first went to live in Jemez I had many more serious things than photographing to think of. I was indeed both safe and comfortable there, but life was not yet to be peaceful for me. There came hurrying one day a rider from across the Rio Grande with a message from the luckless Gus. He wrote :

" The rascals here have seized me and thrown me into the prison, accusing me of certain things which are false, but their real desire is to make away with me in the night over a certain matter, as you may well guess. I beg you to come, and come quickly, and testify for me against their false accusation, and set me free. Only come quickly. You will find a ford opposite Berna-lillo."

It did not take me long to saddle my California mare and ride for the Rio Grande. It was a dark afternoon of autumn as I pushed steadily on through the wide and empty land ; no one lived in this part but a few other pueblo Indians, and I was too anxious about my friend to wait for company. Every one in New Mexico knows that Bernalillo lies at the foot of the great Zandia mountain, a noble landmark ; but that day, as it happened, there was a dense fog over the whole valley, and the Zandia was blotted out. Rain in autumn followed by fog is a thing that does not occur once in a quarter of a century in New Mexico, but as luck would have it this was the one time when it did. Still I knew my general direction, and pressed on, my only fear that of arriving too late. The ford was no matter of trouble, for how easily we had passed the Rio Grande before !

JEMEZ.   THE CHIEFS CONSULTING

Yet as the day darkened, and the failing light proved that the invisible sun must be already setting, it was hard not to feel uneasy about riding an unknown water in darkness.

Suddenly from on ahead came a wild, growling noise in my ears ; it was the voice of angry waters, and in an instant there flashed into my mind that the river had another name, the Rio Brave del Norte, the Fierce River of the North.

I heard a dull roar, and then through the fog there loomed before me a sheet of yellow water racing down from the left. The curtains of the fog hung low, trailing upon the face of the flood ; the baffled eyes could barely see the distance of a stone's cast ; that wan water might be a mile across. I looked for the tracks of horses to show the ford. There were none, for when the river rose with the rain it washed its banks clean.

Yet I was wanted badly on the other side, so, hoping it would be passable somehow, I drove the mare into the stream. Out, out, from the shore we went, and the fog and the dusk closed round us ; the strong stream rose on her left side as she leaned up against the current, so that it banked itself higher there and curled with a hoarse sucking noise round her near shoulder. I drew up my feet till I all but kneeled in the saddle to escape the climbing wave. Looking back, the shore behind was lost in fog ; looking forward, the wished-for land beyond was still invisible. All round were only the trailing curtains of the mist

D

and the fierce River of the North, growling as it swept ever onwards to the Gulf.

And then the mare's hind legs sank under her. I had felt the same thing once before, and knew with a sickening feeling it was the quicksand's grip. "It is all up," I thought; "this is the end." Short time is there for prayer when the quicksand has taken hold. And then right over my head, seemingly from heaven itself, rang out a soft and solemn bell, quite near me. No house, no church was there to be seen, no land for that matter, but through the darkness the bell rang on. I think the call of the bell fairly lifted me up, and lifted the mare too. As if in answer, she made a desperate struggle forwards; her forefeet gained a harder bottom. Another struggle, and the grip of the quicksand on her hind legs suddenly relaxed; she had found her footing once more. The curtains of the fog lifted, and the river bank loomed up, and the old tower of Bernalillo church, sending the call of its vesper bell across the twilight waters. A minute more and we stood safe and dripping on the solid land. The roar of the Fierce River was no longer a terror. I heard only the message of the vesper bell, peace and safety, and the day's work well done. For that same night my friend Gus was a free man again.

CHAPTER IV

CONCERNING BEARS AND RABBITS

THE Jemez Indians were a thoroughly sporting people, and they loved going out on a hunt. They liked the good fresh deer meat, and they also liked the sport. But they did not like to kill every animal. John told me a queer story of how he went out after bear with a couple of Indians from the pueblo, Beneficio and Juan Antonio. " They were willing to go," said John, " but some of the Indians in the pueblo would on no account share in killing a bear. Not, of course, that they were afraid, but there was something peculiar and half sacred about bears, so that killing one could only be atoned for by giving a funeral feast, which comes slightly expensive."

However, Beneficio and Juan Antonio were willing to take the chances of that, and we started out.

" Well, I ran on to three bears, an old one and her two cubs, up there in the sierra, and I saw her before she saw me, for she had her head down in a hole in the ground grubbing away hard after something or other. She had worked herself farther into the hole, too, than I imagined, for when I raised the Winchester and let her have it, as I thought, square in the heart, the bullet struck too far back and only wounded her; she roared with anger at the smart of the bullet, and reared up on her hunkers holding her head high and looking round every way to see what had hit her. And then I did what I've often thought since was a foolish thing; instead of giving her a second shot I was so afraid of losing the cubs that I shot one of them instead, and he squealed, and ran off a little bit and lay down under a bush. If she'd seen me then and come for me we might have had a lively time. But she was thinking more of her cubs than of me, and she dropped on all fours and started for the other one, not regarding a second shot that I gave her, and when she got to the cub she just cuffed it and banged it with both paws, right and left, to make it run away and escape the danger. It did run, too, and went quite a way off, while I gave her another shot that laid her out. But the cub didn't run far, and I went after it, round through the brush, and killed it too.

"So there I had three bears lying dead, all in one place as you may say, and you can bet those two Indians were awful pleased. They knew, of course, that though I'd killed the bears I was going to whack up with them, and when I told them they could have the cubs and the old bear would do for me, they thought it fine. But now

JEMEZ LOOKING ON

here was one of their queer superstitions. Among themselves it is the rule that no matter who kills a bear, the first man who lays a hand on it is the man to whom it belongs, and they were mighty anxious that I shouldn't touch those cubs before they did. So, naturally, I left it to them to touch them first, though whether their notion on the subject has anything to do with the spirit of the dead bear taking any interest in the matter is more than I can say. However, we got the bears properly cut up, and, as we had two horses and four burros along, we had stock enough to pack them all down to the pueblo at one trip.

"But you'd have been surprised to see the reception we got. For when we came near the pueblo, Beneficio and Juan Antonio began firing their guns in a way that carried a signal to the rest of the Indians that they were coming back triumphant with bear. And I think the whole pueblo turned out to meet us, yelling and firing off their guns by way of salute. Crowds of them came, men, women and children, and when they met us and learned that we were bringing in three bears they were mighty jubilant.

"And, if you please, here came old squaws with clubs, and they formed up and walked alongside of the burros, and every once in a while they'd give a whack with a club to one of the dead bears and say rude things to him, to make him understand that it was their innings now, and that he was their meat. And afterwards Beneficio and Juan Antonio had to stand treat, as I said, and were stuck for a feast. But I guess that didn't hurt them much."

But there could be a very different sort of hunt —and that I saw with my own eyes.

" Jack-rabbit hunt to-morrow ! " said my friend Victoriano. " Everybody will be going out to hunt rabbits all day. The horse-herd is being brought down from the sierra this evening on purpose. Where are your boomerangs ? "

"Haven't any," was all I could reply. " Besides, I'm not allowed to go. At least that's what I gathered from the Mexicans."

" Oh, yes, you are," said he, " you're not Español, you're an American, or what comes to the same thing, an Inglés, and you are the honoured guest of the pueblo. We never allow any of the Mexicans to come, but you're different ; you know we treat you as one of ourselves."

" Indeed you do," said I, " and very proud I am of it." Truth to tell, I was flattered by the honour paid me by the very exclusive redmen of the Jemez village community. For I knew with what vigour they kept all outsiders, and Mexicans in particular, severely at a distance.

" Very well," said I, " I'll come. But I don't understand boomerangs and I might hit the wrong man ; some one else might get hurt instead of the rabbits. I'll just bring my gun along." At this proposition, much to my surprise, he put on a look of the utmost horror. How had I put my foot in it now ?

" Hush ! " he said solemnly. " This is a sacred hunt ; this is a matter of religion ; the rabbits are all for the cacique to make ' big medicine ' ; shot rabbits wouldn't do at all. They must be killed with a club or a stone. It would be very wicked to use gunpowder, or even to bring out a gun at all. Everything has to be done strictly according to the rules. You must be ' correct.' "

In the religious ceremonies of the Red Indians " correctness " in details is all-important. The sky would probably fall if you were to offer in sacrifice meal of black corn instead of the orthodox blue colour.

" What nonsense ! " was on the tip of my tongue to say, but it didn't get out. After all, suppose I had deliberately presented myself at a meet of the Quorn with a double-barrel specially loaded for the benefit of the fox, I should have been liable to hear much more sulphurous language than that of my Indian friend.

" All right," I said, " boomerangs it is. What's the fine for knocking over a papoose ? " But he didn't hear the question, for he had run off to his house to fetch my supply of missiles, and was back again with them in a minute.

Boomerangs they were not, though some fanciful ethnologists are pleased to call them so. Real boomerangs are flattened, and bent at a sharp angle, and come from Australia. To my mind, these were like nothing so much as "squailers."

Long ago, my boy friend Johnny Strong when he was at school at Marlborough had taught me how squailers were made and used; they were pieces of tough ash or cane, about a foot and a half long. If you could "bag" a neat walking-stick it cut up into two. And at one end you cast on a lump of lead the size of a very big walnut or a very small egg, and about the same shape. You held your squailer by the small end, and you shied it as hard as you could in the direction of a rabbit or a partridge. If the object aimed at was rash enough to run or fly into the line of the squailer it was a dead rabbit or a dead bird, and it tasted exceedingly good broiled over a fire in Savernake Forest. "The Marquis's gamekeepers did not love us, but we squailed in spite of them," said Johnny Strong.

Remembering Johnny and squailing, I looked forward to an exciting time with the Jemez boomerangs. An I got it, but not exactly as I expected.

The meet next day was on top of a high mesa above the valley. Everybody was there, and in full fig. The men were in their extra-long leggings of red buckskin and their shirts of white cotton, worn not tucked in, but flapping loose outside in true Indian fashion, confined only by a leather belt at the waist. The ladies appeared in beautifully white buckskin leggings under a short skirt of blue blanket. The small children seemed to wear nothing of any consequence except a few strings. A number of the men were on horseback, but the great majority appeared to intend to run down their rabbits on foot. Their wolfish dogs came too, a motley pack, licking their lips in holy eagerness to begin, for a sacred rabbit-hunt didn't come every day. Plenty of cedar and juniper brush grew all about the mesa, and I looked to see the pack sent into cover at once. My mare, bred on the plains of California, was very fresh, and tossed her head in excitement at the prospect of a run.

" Why don't we begin ? " I asked Victoriano. " Why don't the cacique, or whoever bosses this show, throw off ? "

" Hush ! " said he. " There you go again. Can't you see that he's making the sacred fire ? Prayers always before a rabbit-hunt, you know." I noticed now that the mounted men had all got off, and were waiting beside their horses, and the whole assembly was standing still facing the east. A little smoke rose straight up in the air from our front, where two or three of the chiefs were busy, and a sort of litany or invocation in their own language was being recited. I couldn't understand this as I didn't know their lingo. Jemez was so exclusive that it had a language quite unlike that of any other pueblo ; it seemed to consist of long string of gasps, gurgles, and grunts, run together without any stops. I don't believe they could understand it themselves in the dark, without the signs which they used freely to make themselves intelligible.

I asked Victoriano what all this jabber was about anyhow. He put his finger on his lips by way of shocking me into silence. " Don't speak," he murmured. " Cacique is praying to the Shiuana—the spirits—for good luck ; don't speak a word of Spanish now [he and I talked in Spanish], or you'll spoil it all ; only our own language is correct." Of course, I had put my unlucky foot —or, to speak more accurately, my tongue—in it once more.

Prayers over, the fun began. All started off at once in every direction. Rabbits bolted from the bushes, closely chivied by the dogs, and boome-rangs whizzed and rattled against each other all around, amid the excited yells of old and young. But we who were on horseback did not stay long among the infantry ; we galloped forward, and were soon busy on our own account. The top of the mesa was splendid going for horses, but its rocky scarps were as steep as the roofs of a house, and it was intersected here and there by rugged ravines. The California mare was speedy across the flat, but was nowhere over the rough ground alongside of the mountain-bred Indian ponies. Victoriano and I were racing for a rabbit, whose black scut—the Jemez jack-rabbits have black tails, not white—bobbed along only a few yards ahead of us, when a yawning gully opened in our front. Over went the Indian pony like a deer.

No such luck for me ; the mare leaped, blundered, sprawled and rolled over with me. I lay half-stunned for a minute ; those rocks were most uncommon hard ; I scrambled to my feet ; my face was cut and bleeding, and I was shaken pretty severely, but, oh, the condition of the mare's knees ! Ruefully I collected my scattered boomerangs and led her back to the village. Could it have been my ill-timed interruption of the sacred incantation in the tabooed Spanish speech that had brought me this bad luck ? I washed her cuts as well as my own, and plastered and bandaged to the best of my ability. Then, after a rest and a little much-needed " medical comfort," I set out, on foot this time, to the scene of the hunt.

Some parties were already returning with abundant trophies of their success, but the fun on top of the mesa was still going on. Being really hares, these " rabbits " don't burrow or go to ground, so that you can keep on hunting them all day long. I soon found Victoriano, who had killed a brace himself, and had given his horse to his son to ride. He was with a large party of both sexes hunting on foot, and all of them were hallooing lustily whenever a rabbit—they were fewer now—was started by the dogs.

I was on the outskirts of this crowd, when suddenly one of the panting red-mouthed pack sprang into a cedar bush with an eager yelp, and out darted a rabbit almost under my feet. Whiz ! I sent a boomerang at him—whiz ! I sent a second ;

Brer Rabbit either dodged too quick or else my hand had lost its cunning with the squailer—anyhow, I missed. He doubled past me to rush by a squaw fifty yards farther on. Her boomerang whizzed, and over he rolled, a dead rabbit.

"Scored off me that time!" said I, going up to congratulate her; every one crowded round the two of us with merry whoopings; I thought the squaw looked rather shy; the crowd became convulsed with merriment. "Oh, I acknowledge the corn," said I. "So glad you're all pleased."

Victoriano gave me a pat on the shoulder. "Take off that coat," said he. I was wearing a beautiful beaded and fringed buckskin coat. At this I turned a little blue. "What for?" I stammered. At Marlborough, according to Johnny's story, "Take off your jacket" was the ominous preliminary to a brief scene with a head master who could (to quote Henry V) lay on like a butcher. But then at school you were not licked for missing your rabbit, but for killing him, which was poaching.

"What am I to take off my coat for?" I repeated, not without anxiety. Corporal punishment for grown-ups was one of the peculiar institutions of Jemez. With my own eyes I had seen it inflicted.

"Take it off," he reiterated, "be quick, and those things, what you call 'calzon,'" and he pointed to my nether garments. "Make haste; you've got to be first; she's going to take off

JEMEZ SQUAW

hers." I felt frightfully embarrassed. What on earth did they expect me to do? To me it was like a ghastly dream, but the crowd appeared more delighted than ever.

"Can't you understand?" he said irritably. "You've got to be 'correct.' She's killed your rabbit, so you've got to put on her clothes, and she is to put on yours and then you've got to hunt in petticoats till you've killed a rabbit yourself, and then you take your rabbit to her and she gives you back your things."

"Oh, look here," I burst out, "I say, I can't stand that, you know, it wouldn't do."

"But you must," said my friend very anxiously. "Didn't I tell you this is a religious ceremony, this rabbit hunt. Must do all the proper things."

"But it's most improper," said I. "I say, where the dickens is the hunt secretary, or the umpire, or referee, or whatever you call him, who settles these matters? I'm 'not out,' you know. It isn't a case of leg before wicket at all. I want to appeal. And you haven't got the right rules. I know she 'wiped my eye' but what she ought to have is the brush, I mean the pads. I'll give the trophy up to her with pleasure, but not my 'calzon.' Never." But I thought of poor Captain Good in "King Solomon's Mines," and his "beautiful white legs," and shivered with anticipation.

"Nonsense!" said my friend severely. "There's no umpire, or, at least, we're all umpires, and it's given against you, and there's no appeal. Our rules are sacred, and must be obeyed. Look what's happened to you already ; there, you've got your face all cut and scratched. That's because you, most improperly, would speak Spanish at prayers. Off with those ' calzon ' of yours first. She'll put them on and give you hers so as to be ' correct.' " I looked at her white buckskin leggings, and short blue woollen—kilt, shall I say ? —and gasped. " Correct," indeed !

Suddenly a chance of escape offered itself. While the eager crowd had closed round us, determined not to lose a single detail of this most interesting " swop," the red-mouthed hound who had led to my discomfiture by putting up that rabbit under my feet had been busy nuzzling round another cedar bush hard by. Now he made a quick pounce and a scurrying series of grabs, and emerged with a small rabbit kicking in his jaws. Breaking through the crowd, I rushed at him, seized the victim in one hand, and beat him off with the other till he let it go.

" My bird, I think ! " cried I, holding up the prize out of reach of his hungry jaws. Was not this rabbit the captive of my boomerang with which I had clubbed off the dog ? The crowd cheered as I presented it to the squaw, who, I am bound to say, seemed to be immensely relieved. I know that I was.

And thus the sacred rules of the rabbit-hunt were complied with, and we ended up quite " correct." What they were all at is more than I can venture to say; I have heard learned anthropologists talk about totems, and ceremonial slayings of beasts and men: perhaps this was some festivity of the sort. All I know is that, if any rash man wants to go out hunting again with the Jemez Indians on the Feast of St. Bunny, my advice to him is to learn the rules by heart first—all of them, including the peculiar penalties enacted for a miss—and then if he has to come home arrayed in a less dignified garb than he would like—well, at any rate, he cannot lay the blame of his discomfiture upon me.

CHAPTER V

QUAINT indeed as a religious performance did the holy jack-rabbit hunt seem to me, but I discovered that there were certain folks among the Mexicans who could see the quaintest of the Indian shows and go them one better. Practically when I was living in the Indian pueblo with John Miller, I hardly ever went to the Mexican village of Jemez; the memories brought up by the scene of Vicente's murder were too horrible. All the same I had there a few very good friends, but there were also those others whom I knew only too well for deadly enemies. Riding up to Jemez on one of these rare visits of mine I was a little surprised to see quite a crowd standing at one of the entrances to the village, who were clearly spectators keenly watching some affair of very special interest that was going on. So much I could tell from their still, silent, absorbed concentration on the thing, whatever it was.

And then, as I rode near, I was able to see over their heads from the viewpoint of my saddle something that fairly made me sit up. The open space in the middle of the houses was empty save for a procession of six figures; six men stripped to the waist and barefooted, each having the face and head muffled close in a white cotton wrap which hid his identity absolutely. The six walked, stooping forwards half double, with bent knees and long slow dragging steps, one behind the other; each figure held in its two hands a many-thonged scourge made of soap-weed, and at each step the figure raised the hands to the shoulder and brought the scourge sharply down its own back: all the six scourges were red, and the bare backs were red, and the white cotton waist-cloths below were growing red, too, with the blood. Erect and bare-headed with no cotton wrap to hide his face walked in front of the line a man in ordinary clothes. He carried an open book, and his lips mumbled some droning litany or other. Suddenly it flashed across my mind how that very day, just before I started, some Indian in the pueblo had said to me, " Español very mad to-day: do much fool thing to-day." Of course this flagellation was what the Indian had meant. And now I remembered to have read of such things as Flagellant orders as existing away ever so far back in the Middle Ages. Obviously these self-torturers were a survival, and I watched them with redoubled interest.

The spectators in front of me stood there in ordinary dress, nor had they their faces hidden, and the next moment I recognized among them

E

Miterio Archuleta. He was a son of old Francisco Archuleta of the Jemez Hot Springs who with all his family were always our good friends ; they had no sort of use for poor old Vicente's brutal murderers. I signed to Miterio, and he came up and put his hand on my saddle and we talked.

" What's all this business ? " I asked him in a low voice.

" You no sabe ? " returned he with surprise. " These are the Penitentes." Of course he too dropped his voice so as not to be overheard, for we spoke Spanish.

" But who and what are they ? " I said. " And why do they do it ? Do you know them yourself ? "

" Oh, no," he returned, " though I can make a pretty good guess. They are a secret society and they flog themselves thus every year. They meet in a big room they have in one of the houses here, and they know each other by secret signs and passwords ; they call themselves Hermanos, Brothers, and it is quite true that they have their lodges all over New Mexico. They take it in turns to flog themselves, and when their turn comes there is no backing out ; they have got to take it. But I believe it only comes to each brother once in a few years. Probably half these men that you see here now looking on in ordinary clothes belong to the Society and have taken their turn. I couldn't swear to it ; I never was a Penitente, me, but I feel sure enough about them. This is how they are supposed to expiate their sins : perhaps Vicente's murderers are expiating theirs here and now."

Wonderful, incredible almost, is the mystery of human nature ! That men should be capable of an atrocious crime and capable also of submitting to this extremity of self-torture as some sort of atonement for it ! I felt utterly staggered.

"They won't be moved to confess their sins, I suppose," said I. "They won't give themselves away to the civil law."

"But you don't understand," said the Mexican. "This has nothing to do with the law. This is part of religion. It is all quite different. It may be that they will go out of the pueblo to the Calvary there on the hill and there they may crucify one of them as a sort of a sin-offering. But the law, never."

"Crucify him ? " I exclaimed.

"Yes," he answered, "crucify him, with cords, that is, not with nails. You know at the Calvary there are three or four crosses made out of heavy wood poles cut from trees. They may tie him, the one chosen, or it may be the one who offers himself for sacrifice, to a cross and set it there upright with him on it for hours and do their flogging of themselves round it. But that's not done often and I don't know if they will try that to-day. As I told you, I'm not a Penitente, me, and I'm not in their secrets and no one out-side the society can know about what they intend to do."

" But does the man crucified die ? " I asked.

" No," he returned, " not very often, that is. They take him down before it gets as bad as that, only there are times when they are too late and then there's nothing for it but to bury him."

" And there's no inquest, nor nothing ? " I said. " It's all hushed up ? "

" Why, of course," he said. " Didn't I say that all this is religion and quite outside the law. Why, the very man whose duty it would be to set the law in motion here is one of the biggest men among the Penitentes. That much I know myself. Do you fancy he would do anything against his brothers in religion ? "

I felt the hopelessness of the position.

" If you wait a little," said Miterio, " there may be some women coming out. They do it too sometimes."

" Never ! " I exclaimed horror-struck. " Look here. I must say good-bye. I'm going back to the pueblo. I want to talk to John Miller. I never dreamed of anything like this."

" Well, good-bye," said the friendly Mexican. " Come and see us at the Hot Springs when you can." And with no more ado I turned my mare and rode straight back again to Jemez. And

JEMEZ CEREMONIAL DANCE HELD IN THE PUEBLO. DANCERS IN TWO LINES FACING EACH OTHER. MEN WEAR WREATHS AND FOX SKINS. WOMEN WOODEN HEAD DRESSES WITH PLUMES. BEHIND IS SACRED BOOTH COVERED WITH BLANKETS

there John Miller, who knew a thing or two about New Mexico, confirmed every word Miterio had said.

As a contrast to this mediæval performance of Flagellants which I actually saw myself, I will describe an Indian dance which I did not see but which a trustworthy eye-witness told me of. As a Christian of Spanish descent my Mexican friend held himself to be a White Man and very far above mere Indian savages. These dances are not unknown to anthropologists, but it is seldom that any stranger is admitted to see them. " I only tell the tale as 'twas told to me." If I had to give it a title I should call it " Worshippers of Nature."

It was a summer's night, with the great broad shield of a full moon swinging low across the southern sky. The deep shadow of the pines fell as an inky blackness all round the " abra," or park-like opening in the woodland ; but over the middle of the opening itself was shed a flood of silver light that made the glowing fire of willow wood there burn lurid and yellow. No common fire was this ; it was sacred, because it made part of the ritual of a sacred dance, and a great caldron simmered over the coals, watched by one solitary grey-haired priest.

Two red men with towering masks, weirdly painted, that half hid their faces and rose like lofty helmets over their heads, had peremptorily stopped the White Man and his companion at the edge of the abra, and were sharply questioning their intrusion.

For the White Man's warning they had put finger on lip as an emphatic requirement from him of absolute silence, while in low earnest tones they interrogated his companion in the tongue of the Indians.

The White Man did not understand the words, but he knew that his companion was explaining that he did not intrude thus upon their most sacred rite without special permission. These two masked guards held buffalo spears in their hands, and the sharp steel at the end was significantly red. Quick death was the measure ready to be meted out to rash violators of the mysteries.

Civilization seemed very far off from this lone spot in the wild wood, and these ancient sanctities of their race were not to be trifled with. But the White Man's credentials were good, and with reiterated signs of caution the guards went back to their posts, and the White Man and his companion advanced to the fire.

Once admitted thus, and safe within the ring of guards, he felt almost as though he were himself already becoming one of the initiate, though he was still ignorant of what was to come. He had been promised that his eyes should see their most sacred rite, but precisely in what it consisted he had not been told, although strange whispers had reached his ear. He stood here upon the threshold of the unknown, and the sense of mystery deepened till it filled his very soul.

The old priest looked up from the cauldron he was stirring. A red fillet bound his forehead, and snaky grey locks flowed down from under it. His seamed and wrinkled face gazed gloomily now at this new-comer of an alien race.

"Be sure you do not speak to him," muttered the White Man's companion. "Remember that he is sacred here; he is working the things that belong to the world of the spirits; he may not be touched or spoken to by any who are unconsecrated, or Those Above will be angry, and everything will go wrong. Leave it all to me."

The White Man was no stranger to the belief of his Red brothers in the real actual presence among them of supernatural beings: he knew well that it was their absolute conviction that victory and defeat, joy and woe, aye, all that can make life worth having or death terrible were in unseen hands; to propitiate Those Above— no easy art—was the Key of Life; to offend them was ruin and destruction. And knowing this belief of theirs he understood the weight of the injunction, and his lips were closed.

His companion took a strange powder from the pouch on his belt and tossed it into the fire as he invoked the Spirits of the Air and of the Earth. He slipped a pinch into the White Man's hand.

" This for you," he whispered. " Do the same."

The White Man glanced curiously at the magic stuff in his hand ; then casting it as he was bid upon the coals, he saw it flash and sparkle brightly ere it was consumed.

" The offering is accepted," said his companion aloud ; " the spirits are not angry. You may stay ; " and he looked across at the old grey priest, whose gloom changed suddenly to a smile as he signed to the dancers to begin again.

The monotonous tom-tom-tomming of the drums recommenced, and the lines were reformed. In the middle of the abra the light of the fire, as well as of the moon, was poured upon the shining bronze bodies of a great company of folk.

These were the true Americans indeed, the ancient children of the soil. And in all that company there were none who were not in the prime of life. There were no grey-heads present, save the old priest alone, and he stood beside his cauldron apart from the company of dancers. Rhythmically the bronze bodies swung and swayed and the flashing feet rose and fell, as the inter-rupted rites were renewed. Armlets and anklets they wore of green juniper, deftly woven round each limb, light and feathery, quivering in the motion.

Clothing they had none, save that each man bore the untrimmed spotted pelt of some small beast of chase hanging lightly below his waist ;

and the bushy tail and the little pads that had once been feet jerked and bobbed fitfully in response to the motions of the splendid lithe figure of the dancer.

The firelight gave but an uncertain glow, yet it was enough to mark the eager purpose and the high-strung exaltation that shone in the wild dark faces as they leapt and danced. They were in truth a goodly company, the warriors of the tribe.

Yes, these were warriors all, with no immature lads among them : they were bold fighting men every one ; but to-night they were not in warrior's array ; to-night there was no war-paint on their faces, and this was no war-dance that they had come to hold up here in the mountain-forest afar from their village.

The White Man had heard (as I have said) strange whispers of the rite they celebrated every year at that critical season, when the seeds have been entrusted to the keeping of the teeming earth, but the harvest is not yet ; a rite held not in honour of the blood-besmeared god of battle and slaughter, but of Her, the Great Mother, by whose power the kindly fruits of the earth awake into being and yield their increase. It was to win her favour that here in the ivory moonlight resounded the passionate throbbing of the drums and the quick, light patter of the moccasined feet ; and it was because she, the Bringer of Life, was to be worshipped that the glow of the sacred fire shone not on the glancing bodies of warriors alone.

Opposite to their line was a second row of dancers, and this second row consisted of the women of the tribe. In their case, as in that of the men, youthful immaturity and wrinkled age were alike absent : all without exception looked to be in the very flower and prime of life.

The dance had but just begun, and there was a manifest solemnity in the expression and in the action of the celebrants ; it was in no trivial spirit that these folk engaged in the mysteries of their religion.

The two rows of men and women stood facing each other, some thirty yards apart, and each hand clasped the hand next it at a half-arm's length, and all together they flung the linked hands skyward as if to invoke the powers above.

Then with a continuous downward sweep the clasped hands descended until they almost touched the earth, in appeal, as it might seem, to the powers beneath ; and with that earthward sweep of the hands the lines drew towards each other, and they bent low as if in deep adoration before some invisible altar. And all the time, almost drowning the thrilling rattle of the drums, there rose from the long swaying lines a wild chant, with unknown words and monotonous minor intervals that seemed as elemental as the song of birds.

It was hardly to be called music, and yet it held the secret of all music in it.

There was a marvellous unity in the motions of so great a company of people ; whilst keeping time to that strange song and to the beat of the loud drums they bent forward to the earth, and then, raising themselves again, flung up their hands once more to the pale stars that shone overhead. At each prostration their advancing lines seemed about to meet, but at each elevation of the hands they recoiled back again to where they stood before.

In that alternation of advance and retreat, in that contrast of the bold upward sweep of uplifted bodies and of outstretched arms, followed by the free downward swing, and the reverential deep obeisance, there was a mesmeric force that began to send strange thrills along the nerves of the White Man, growing stronger every moment as with fascinated gaze he watched the rapidly increasing fervour of the celebrants.

Louder and louder beat the drums, wilder was the chant, deeper were the prostrations, and swifter the upward spring of the dancers. Closer and closer swung the lines to one another, as each forward rush and each recoil left the distance between them less than it had been.

The two lines drew together by an irresistible law. Wilder and wilder grew the throbbing of the drums, quicker and quicker in answer to them flew the feet of the dancers.

The very air seemed charged with mystic force as if a spirit unseen hovered over this opening in the wildwood, and touched all hearts with its maddening impulse. There was a magic in the ebb and flow of this human tide, flung forward and back by some nameless spell; there was a throb pulsing through that wild elemental chant that burst upon the astonished air, which made the White Man's pulses leap.

Before he came he had but half believed the tales he had heard among the Spanish-speaking folk about this ceremony which was so carefully hidden from them. Their hints of what was the essence of it had seemed too wildly incredible to be aught but the inventions of fancy.

But now, of a sudden, right here in this lone spot hung all around with the dark curtain of the pinewood, and overarched by the starlit canopy of the half-tropic night, nothing was beyond belief, nothing seemed impossible.

Faster and faster came the nerve-stirring rattle of the drums, and the loud notes of the chant went to a swifter measure; more and more rapidly the lines of the dancers swung to and fro, as if approaching a breathlessly expected crisis, from which, nevertheless, something still held them back, like racers plunging madly before a race, yet restrained until the signal should be given by an invisible hand on the reins.

Above their heads against the moonlit sky waved the solemn dark tops of the pines. Behind them in the abra spread a wide tangled thicket of willow-brush; the slender, feathery clusters grew thick to more than twice the height of a man, and met atop, and interwove themselves into a sea of foliage ; but low down between the willow-clusters the wild deer of the mountains had for untold ages come and gone at will, and kept their passways clear, so that in and out through the brush ran dark leafy corridors innumerable, dark with a darkness that neither the broad moon nor the sparkle of the fire-flames lit with a single ray.

Around, outside all, the figures of spearmen were dimly seen, and these were the masked and helmeted guards.

The old grey priest beside the fire stirred the cauldron, and now the words of an incantation rose from his muttering lips. Was it a blessing that he was calling down ? Perhaps. Who shall say ?

Suddenly went up a yell that made the watcher's heart stand still. The long swaying line of women was gone. It melted into a fluid-flickering crowd darting every way to vanish in the willow thickets. After them dashed the men, and all were instantly lost and swallowed up in the dusky bowers and recesses of that leafy labyrinth.

For a minute was seen the waving of willow tops, and the rustling of parting boughs was heard yielding to the press of bodies. Then came stillness absolute.

The open place, a moment before so thronged with dancers, stood there empty and bare : the maddening throb of the drums had ceased, and no sound broke the silence but the voice, earnestly uplifted, of the old grey priest. His words were strong, urgent, insistent, as of one who will not be denied.

"He is speaking to Those Above," whispered the White Man's companion; "he is asking for all the good things: that the maize may fill and ripen; that the wheat may be fat and full of meat; that our kine may bear calves, and the mares bring forth strong foals; that the Great Mother may be kind to the young things and give them nourishment, and that the race of the red men fail not from off the face of the earth.

"He asks all this; he asks very earnestly. It is right that he should ask, and it is right that the red men should do the things that are pleasing to the Spirits of Power.

"If they are unkind we die and cease to be, and speedily the red men must fade away and perish; but we do all that lies with us to do to keep the race alive, and the good spirits who love the red men, they of the old long-ago days and the times of our forefathers, they will hear us when we seek to serve them thus, and will bless us with abundant increase."

The White Man looked up at the silent stars above, and there came to him a sudden sense that he was truly initiate now; it seemed to him for a moment as if the inmost heart of things lay open and unveiled. His mind dived deep into the past, to reappear, as it were, after that plunge, and breathe another air : the larger, fresher air of an earlier day.

The present world fell away from him, and other strange fantastic worships whose memory lives only in ancient story took shape before his newly-illumined senses.

Here in the abra the inner meaning of many things that had been formerly enigmas to him was flashed upon his mind.

" Do not speak to them when they return," whispered his companion. " Remember that they are sacred. They will come close to us here to drink the cup at the hands of the priest, but they are sacred to Those Above, and are not to be touched or handled or spoken to by others who are unconsecrated."

Suddenly from the pines on the right came a sound of flapping wings, and a great night-bird slid heavily off the boughs of a tree whence it had been looking down on the strange nocturnal invasion of its solitary domain ; slowly, with long wing-beats, it soared its way across the abra, crossing right above the sacred fire, and then disappeared through the pine columns on the left.

" An omen," cried the grey old priest, " an omen of good ! The bird of the night has heard us, and is kind."

A rustling was heard once more among the willow boughs, and two and two the dancers began to come forth, making for the fire in the centre and the priest.

The White Man plucked his companion by the arm, and whispered, " Let us go." He had seen a strange thing, and he had divined yet more than he had seen.

The Mexican's tale carried me back into the far far past. I had read my classics and remembered stories of strange rites and ceremonies in the old days of Greece and Rome, but I felt that I had never understood them so well as now. Already the sight of the self-torturing Penitentes bearing their heavy crosses, with' their bleeding backs and their dropping scourges, had carried me centuries back, for in beholding those terrible Flagellants I had beheld the very spirit of the Dark Ages incarnate. But in this tale of the nature dance of the red men, the primitive children of the soil, I had been permitted a glimpse into the dark soul of Paganism itself.

That glimpse was practically the only one I got of the deeper side of Paganism in New Mexico.

Though nominally Christian they had a sacred place in their pueblo, the estufa, which no white man had ever entered, but of which the Mexicans told dark stories, probably untrue.

I never asked any questions or intruded in any way on their special customs. Now and then

JEMEZ, CEREMONIAL DANCE. CHORUS ADVANCING AND SINGING. WANDBEARERS IN FRONT. HELD BY DAYLIGHT IN THE PUEBLO

they would say to John and me, " You no come out to-day," and then we religiously kept our door shut. They treated me with hospitality ; I could only return it by courtesy.

F

CHAPTER VI

HOW JEMEZ GOT ITS WATER

"WELL, what's your little game?" I inquired of my friend Victoriano as I saw him saddling his horse with an expression of extreme solemnity on his face, while he stood before his house-door in the Jemez pueblo. That the Indians of the pueblo had some business or other on hand was plain, because the horse herd had been brought in and a number of their ponies with lassos round their necks were standing before their respective masters' doors and undergoing the process of saddling likewise.

But my worthy redskin friend only turned his back on me with a shake of his head, and drew his cinch a full three inches tighter till the roan pony grunted and tried to bite him.

"Got another sacred jack-rabbit hunt on?" said I. "Want to try to make me swop clothes with a squaw again? Wire in, if you do; I'll take my chances that you don't score."

I had thought to get a laugh out of him by this reminiscence, but he only looked more solemn than ever as he went on pulling at the

66

JEMEZ, SQUAW CARRYING WATER

cinch. When he had drawn it so tight that his pony had a waist like a wasp and could only stand on the tips of his toes, he eyed me rather queerly and said in a half-whisper :

" We going to make San Joaquin give us rain."

Undoubtedly Jemez wanted rain. Sere, yellow and parched lay the mesas and valleys all around, beneath the burning New Mexican sun, now at this season when they should have been green with springing grass. Nay, worse still, the river itself, the rushing Rio Jemez, that ought to have flushed their *acequia madre*[1] till it ran brimming full and copiously watered the corn and beans and wheat of these industrious red men, had shrunk to a mere fraction of its proper size, and left their all-important irrigating channels as dry as so many dusty footpaths. Their crops were withering fast, and there would be grievous hunger next winter in the pueblo for all, even for those fat little imps of copper-coloured children who were now rolling and wallowing, naked and happy, in a playground they had never enjoyed before, namely, the dry bottom of the main ditch.

A week before this they had tried the effect of a solemn procession up the cañon, to their great and adored patroness, Santa Margarita, who, according to the myth current among them, had saved the lives of their forefathers from the fury of the Spanish soldiers by catching them in mid-air as they hurled themselves despairingly from

[1] Main ditch.

the cliff-brow, and had planted them safely down here at Jemez and protected them ever since. But on this occasion she had failed them, and the terrible drought still went on.

Nor was she their sole resource. Ever since it began they had never ceased for a day to lay their humble offerings and their fervent, passionate prayers at the feet of their other patron saint, San Joaquin, who stood, a somewhat tawdry and bedizened life-size wooden figure, in his little chapel on the outskirts of the pueblo.

When Victoriano said, " Make San Joaquin give us rain," in that mysterious half-whisper, I felt that he had something out of the common in his mind.

" Oh, do let me come too," I entreated. " Is it to be a horseback procession ? I want to see what you do to propitiate San Joaquin."

The pious redskin seemed to relent a little.

" All right ; you get your horse ; come along."

Five minutes later I was mounted on my California mare and tearing along towards the chapel, in the rear of a galloping crowd of excited red men. Just outside the chapel door we halted, and shouts went up, " Have him out ! lasso him ! drag him down ! down to the river with him, and duck him well ; we'll give him plenty of water if he won't give us any ! " Two or three Indians dismounted and ran in ; there was a confused scuffling inside, the end of a lasso was chucked out through the open door, caught by a mounted Indian, and made fast to the horn of his saddle. He wheeled his horse, struck him hard with the quirt, and started away on the keen jump. Fast to the other end of that lasso, out through the open door with a jerk and a bound, came that long ungainly wooden doll they called San Joaquin. The tawdry finery had been stripped off it, the choking noose had been looped tight around its neck, and here it flew along in the dust, bobbing and twisting madly in the rear of the flying horseman like a tin kettle tied to a dog's tail. The rider headed for the river, the Indians raced after, and I, unheeded, joined in as a spectator. A young buck, whirling the end of his riata round his head, urged his horse up till he was striding alongside the tormented form of the unhappy saint, and whack—whack—whack—the rope's end descended again and again on the body of that luckless doll. San Joaquin was getting it very hot indeed amid the frantic yells of his maddened worshippers. Really I had to feel quite sorry for him.

"Queer thing, this, to be a part of their religion!" I murmured to myself as I listened to those yells. The old Adam was cropping out through the veneer of skin-deep Christianity!

Splash—we charged fetlock-deep through the sparse runnels of water that meandered here and there through the bed of the Jemez river; the bed, that is to say, where the river ought to have been, for, in fact, the larger half of it was now a waste of barren gravel bars and sand.

Down amid the sand and slush, in among the heels of the panting ponies, the besmeared saint rolled and wallowed, under showers of curses loud and fierce, and a hurricane of blows from rawhide ropes and quirts. I beheld my pious friend Victoriano ride up and smack him hard over the mouth with his heavy whip. "Ah, rascal, rogue, ruffian," he cried, "you take our offerings and you hear us praying all day and yet you give us nothing. I'll teach you to behave so. Take that—and that—and that," and he lashed the object of his devotion with all the power of his vigorous arm. Not a word did I venture to say. I durst not chaff him now. Red Indians under strong religious excitement are kittle cattle to deal with.

And then they took him up, and, wonder of wonders, they carried him back, they wiped him dry, they cleaned him up nicely and dressed him in his own proper garments, and they set him up again in his shrine, and worshipped him harder than ever. They were a highly unaccountable people at Jemez.

Only one short month before I had beheld them laughing consumedly, with many scornful gibes, over the spectacle of their Mexican neighbours, the fanatic Penitentes of Cabralcito, flogging their own bare backs as a penance for their sins till the blood ran down to their heels. "Big fools those Penitentes," this very Victoriano had declared in my hearing, "heap big fools to whip themselves like that—*Español muy loco*—Spaniard very mad!"

And now, here he was whipping the naughtiness out of his own misbehaving saint, poor San Joaquin, on a very similar principle; though there was one highly important difference in his practice, namely, that it was decidedly less painful to the party chiefly concerned.

Later, when I got back to civilization and learned some ethnology, I became aware that it was precious lucky for me that the Jemez Indians had considerably modified their old pagan customs. Now they were satisfied with San Joaquin for a scapegoat. In the good old days it would have been a stranger, possibly me, who would have been roped and beaten and finally very thoroughly drowned to bring water to the waste lands. It was just as well that more modern views penetrated even to the pueblos.

But neither the whipping nor the worshipping seemed to produce the desired effect upon San Joaquin's disposition to come to the relief of his devotees, for a whole week went by and still the river went on shrinking, and still the heavens were as brass.

As a rain-maker the saint proved a flat failure, and the disappointed Victoriano sadly admitted as much. He had sobered off after his excitement, and was now in a calmer mood.

" But what are you going to do about it ? " I inquired. " Haven't you another card, an ace, or a left bower, or something, up your sleeve ? "

He gave me a nod full of meaning. " We have other things we can do," he said, " much stronger than what we do with San Joaquin. But we don't talk about them to everybody."

" You don't propose to discipline me, I hope," was my alarmed response.

But the red man only shook his head more mysteriously than ever. The secrets of their own old religion were too sacred for me; nevertheless, all the same the drought went on. Day by day the strings of patient squaws who marched in single file, each with her water jar balanced on her head, found less water in the pools of the river-beds, and the men's faces grew more and more anxious as they watched the cloudless sky. Then one day I saw with surprise that the biggest ollas were being borne on their heads down to the river, and all day long the women passed up and down the trail that led from it to the village, and instead of their using up the water in their daily washing and cooking it was stored in innumerable jars on the level eaves of the flat-roofed houses along the village streets. Rows upon rows of jars there were, and every one of them brimming full. Meanwhile the young men had gone off to the high sierra and fetched down the horse herd again, a couple of hundred long-maned, long-tailed Indian ponies, and put

SQUAWS FETCHING WATER

them in the corrals outside the villages. The
horses were fat, for there had been rain up in the
high sierra, and the grass up there was green.
When evening came, and every jar in the village
stood full of water on the roofs where the squaws
had assembled, the men retired to the corrals,
and stripped to their waist-cloths ; they sprang
on to their bare-backed ponies with nothing but
a string tied to the lower jaw to guide them ; the
corral bars were thrown open, and with wild yells
the whole troop swept down upon the village,
and, then, what shrieking and excitement on the
part of the squaws !

Up to the house where I was standing dashed
a wild pony with two young men and a small
boy clinging to his back, the boy on his withers,
and one of the men all but slipping off his tail.

" Water wanted," they cried in the Indian
tongue, " much water wanted ; " and much water,
sure enough, they got.   For in a deluge on top
of them water rained from the house-eaves as the
squaws, squealing in their eagerness, turned olla.
after olla upside down over their heads.   Their
wet skins shone like gleaming bronze as they
cried, " Thanks, much thanks," and dashed away
to another house in quest of another shower bath.
For full twenty minutes the fun went on ; the
dripping ponies seemed to share in the excitement, and scampered off from house to house,
and from deluge to deluge, as if they enjoyed it.
Pools of water stood on the hard earth, and

splashed up in showers under their pattering hoofs. It was a grand function for them as well as for their masters.

At last the deluges died away to dribbles ; the stock of water so laboriously collected during the day seemed to be about exhausted, and the ponies and their well-soused riders raced away back to the corrals from which they had come. I stepped out of the doorway from which I had been watching the strange scene, and was picking my way around the house to see if there was any of the fun still going on round the corner, when— whoosh ! I was ducked from head to foot with the contents of a five-gallon olla discharged from above. I looked up, and there was the broad, jolly, laughing face of Reys, the squaw from whom my partner and I rented our rooms, looking down at me.

" Hah ! " she cried gleefully. " The paleface himself has been ducked. Now will the water-spirits make for us much rain."

So they did apparently. You may explain it any way you like, but next day the drought broke up, and we were blessed with a magnificent downpour. And those primitive rainmakers of Jemez were quite satisfied that this was the result of their performance. What could be clearer than that the spirits of the water which the squaws fetched from the river and poured from the eaves had called down the spirits of the waters that were above the firmament, and that their call had been obeyed ? Anyhow they had got me this time, the stranger had been ducked, and the effect was all that could be desired. And for my part, I didn't see exactly how to disprove the Indians' theories.

At the same time, the belief in their own rain-making powers didn't prevent them from being very grateful when my partner, John, who was a skilled miner, blasted away some rocks for them up at the head of their ditch, and thereby doubled their permanent supply of water.

CHAPTER VII

OUR HUNT IN THE SIERRA

"SAY," said John one day, "what's the matter with having another hunt? We're getting short of meat. I don't like killing the wild cattle up there, because the Indians call them the children of the cattle of the Indians, and that makes them a bit jealous. But there's a plenty deer."

"Right you are," said I, "let's go." I had traded with the Indians for a beautiful little sorrel mule which they had bred from one of their pony mares. I called him Captain Jinks and we took him along to pack in any meat we might get.

Accordingly we saddled up and off we went; Keno, of course, went with us, and presently we found ourselves camped high up in the Sierra San Antonio, not very far below timberline. We had tethered the horses to their picketpins in a little mountain meadow hard by, and our tent was pitched on a bank just above a mountain stream. A small fine rain came on after supper, and we crept into our blankets, each man with his Winchester for bedfellow, and Keno was snugly tucked away, too, at John's feet. Out

R. B. TOWNSHEND IN THE SIERRA ABOVE JEMEZ

of deep sleep we came broad awake, roused by a warning bark from Keno under the blankets. We listened and we heard our terrified horses rushing round their picketpins. Keno was still too lazy to turn out. " Bow-wow-wow," he went, however, as if to say to John, " You get up, boss. There's something going on round here."

Suddenly we heard, quite close to us, short angry puffs like an engine blowing off steam. It was the hoarse " wough-wough " of a grizzly bear. In a moment we were up on our knees and peering out of the tent front, rifle in hand. It was as dark as a wolf's throat : literally, you couldn't see your hand held out before your face. The fine rain had put out the fire, there was no moon, and the sky was black with clouds. Swiftly John collared Keno, who had at last condescended to get up, and was now, of course, frantic to go and tackle friend Ephraim, as hunters call the grizzly. Our visitor was running backwards and forwards just in front of the tent, fairly snorting with rage at our intrusion of his haunts. Would he come for us ? That was the question. If he did, we two, unable to take any sort of aim in the darkness were likely to have a sorry time of it. Keno, struggling in John's grip, barked a furious defiance. The indignant bear, uncertain what to do, blew off steam, so to speak, more fiercely than ever. The horses, snorting loudly, were making rushes so violent that every moment we expected them to break loose. If he had only known it that bear certainly had us on toast.

Talk of the beasts of the field fearing the majesty of man ! That depends. Wherever men carry good rifles and can handle them, the wild beasts soon learn to run. But, where the men are poorly armed and do not take the offensive, the beast of the field gets as bold as brass. The Mexican shepherds seldom had anything but an old rejected musket, and the bears used to follow the great travelling herds of sheep around in the most presumptuous and familiar manner, paying them night visits with a view to mutton for supper. They got the mutton, too, pretty often, and it was seldom they got a digestive pill in the shape of a musket ball, as the shepherds usually only tried to drive the bears off with torches and stones and shouts and the barking of their dogs. Consequently the bears felt pretty big ; this bear who had disturbed us certainly did. He had come round after mutton, and was very angry at finding we weren't Mexican shepherds, and hadn't any mutton for him. He might have helped himself to a horse, but he couldn't be bothered with horse, a large, rude, awkward thing to sup off with a horrid habit of kicking out violently behind. As for supping off us, well, I never heard of a bear turning man-eater. Possibly " Ephraim " thinks we taste too strong of plug tobacco, at least that is the complaint that South Sea cannibals make of British sailors as a dish, and the Far Western hunter would be equally

flavoured with it. The morning after friend
Ephraim had paid us this visit we set off to return
the call. There was not much difficulty in dis-
covering which way Old Ephraim had gone, for
his tracks were plain in the soft earth ; they were
the biggest bear-tracks we had ever seen, and we
measured them a good fifteen inches from claw
to heel. We each of us carefully inserted fifteen
cartridges in the magazines of our Winchesters,
and then slipped into the firing-chamber a special
cartridge that we only used upon occasion. These
last carried a bullet hollowed out at the point
for a good quarter of an inch, with an empty
closed copper tube inserted in the hole. As we
followed Old Ephraim's trail we soon saw that,
when he did go, he had left in a hurry. Probably
Keno's barking had scared him thoroughly ; anyway, he had dashed headlong through the spruce
timber, kicking up the earth like a galloping
horse. We followed him for miles, but in vain,
till it was plain that he had left for parts unknown,
and we were never likely to see him again in that
country.

" You didn't have old Keno at him last night,"
I said.

" No," answered John ; " I didn't set him on
that time. I was always very shy of letting old
Keno go at a bear. I was afraid the dog might
rush in and get his bulldog grip on to the bear
and that then the bear would kill him. But I
did let him have a go in at a bear once, and this

was how it was. I was out with Keno after deer when I caught sight of a bear on a rocky hill-side about a hundred yards off. I fired at him and knocked him down, but he got up again and ran off up the hill. I fired at him again as he ran, and broke his hind leg, and that rather crippled him, and he ran under a cedar bush and lay down.

"I couldn't see to shoot him again from where I was, so thought I'd let Keno try what he could make of bear, and I sent him after him. Old Keno, he rushed up the hill after the bear in a mighty hurry, but when he came where he was the bear raised his head and opened his great jaws, and gnashed his teeth and roared at him. And Keno looked at him very much surprised, and then he turned and came running back to me, and looked up at me as if to say, 'Boss, is it all right? This is a mighty curious kind of deer you've wounded.'"

"So I came along with him, and when I got close I finished the bear with another shot, and then I encouraged Keno to take hold. And when he understood that I hadn't made any mistake, and that the bear was really what we were after, he ran and took hold of him and woolled him good. You know how strong a bulldog can pull when he gives that muscular twist with his body; well, Keno tugged at the bear like that, and as the bear was lying on the steep hill-side the body gave to his pull and began to slip.

"And I guess that made Keno think the bear

was alive still, and he worried away at him like fury. And the bear came slithering down and slid right on top of Keno so that he lay on him. And the dog just thought he was having the biggest kind of a fight, a hundred times bigger than ever he'd had in Santa Fe, when that bear lay on top of him ; and you'd have laughed to see him claw his way out from underneath the bear, and round on him again and seize him and younk him further down the hill till I had to stop it for fear he'd spoil the hide. Oh, he'd have tackled a bear all right next time, but when I came to think it over I concluded not to risk it."

Just as he had reached this conclusion John noticed that Keno was snuffing the air as if he smelt something. "I believe there are deer close round." said he quietly to me. "We'd better stand still here a minute and let the dog range round. He's cunning as they make 'em, and he's liable to drive 'em right on to us. Off you go, Keno."

Away went Keno into the brush—we were in young spruce—and we two stood back to back, perfectly motionless, with our rifles at the ready. Two men standing thus need not hide themselves in order to get game to come within shot. Back to back, their eyes command the whole circuit around them ; and while they stand stock still, with their rifles sticking out, the deer will take no more heed of them than they would of an old dead tree stump. Some minutes passed thus, when suddenly through the brush we saw the forms of a band of mule deer, which Keno had started, flitting silently past. My partner whistled shrill ; the deer all stopped for an instant. "One, two, three," whispered John (that was a little dodge we had for firing together) and bang went our rifles at the same moment. I had fired at a young buck not more than twenty-five yards away ; I saw the blood start over his heart, and throwing in another cartridge from the magazine I followed him with the sights as he bounded forward, but did not pull trigger. He made the three biggest bounds I ever saw a deer make and then fell dead. If I was not afraid of being accused of telling travellers' tales I would say that every bound was thirty feet. I ran in and bled him, and on opening him I was amazed at the vitality that in spite of the wound had enabled him to make such mighty leaps. The hollow bullet had struck on a rib on the near side, and the compression of the air had caused it to explode ; the lead had burst into fifty pieces, which all struck forward ; they cut the heart absolutely into mincemeat, and two fragments of the bullet had broken two of the ribs on the off side. And yet the animal had been able to make those amazing bounds.

I went over to where John was cleaning his quarry, for his shots had gone home too, and he had killed a deer ; but how differently his bullet had behaved ! He had hit a doe at about eighty yards in the neck. The soft lead had stripped back from the central copper tube and formed itself into a mushroom. We found it lying flattened against the skin on the far side of the neck, having torn its way through the soft tissues and blood-vessels so as to cause instant death, and the doe had fallen in her tracks. Where the bullet went in was a wound that hardly admitted the little finger ; but on the opposite side when the skin was moved was a hole you could shove all four fingers in together. His bullet had expanded ; mine had exploded ; yet they were precisely similar bullets, shot with exactly the same charge of powder from sister rifles. The only difference was that in one case the air in the hollow part of the bullet was so violently compressed on striking the rib that it acted as an explosive ; in the other the air managed to escape among the tissues and the bullet merely expanded without flying into pieces. And the expanding bullet had dealt swifter death than the exploding one.

This certainly was not a long hunt of John's and mine, for we lost no time in dressing our deer and packing them on Captain Jinks, and by nightfall we were back once more at our quarters in the pueblo.

CHAPTER VIII

MUCH as I loved living among the friendly redskins and going for hunts up in the sierra with John, the time came when I was to leave these joys for a very different sort of game. Far away as we were in the remote pueblo of Jemez from direct contact with civilization, nevertheless news did slowly trickle through various channels and get to us at last. And thus it came about that stories reached us from Colorado that there was a really big rush of men looking for gold in the San Juan country, and some of these prospectors were said to have struck it. Naturally, he and I grew more and more restless, and the idea of having a try there ourselves became an obsession with us.

"Of course, you and me don't need to go all the way round by Colorado," said John. "We can go straight up through the Navajo country."

I have already said that John bore no grudge against the Navajo nation generally for the killing of his brother but only against the actual murderers. The San Juan River runs both in Colorado and New Mexico, crossing the borderline more than once. All that wild country up there was still unsurveyed, i.e. no U.S. surveyors had as yet run their lines over it and cut it up into six-mile square townships and one-mile square sections, though the main river courses were sketched out on the maps issued by the railroads. Eagerly we discussed our plans, and ended by making up our minds to try our luck for gold.

"I'll be able to fix up so as I can leave Jemez easily for three months," said John, "and then I can come back here for winter, that is always supposing you and me don't strike it rich."

"We may meet Gus up there," said I. "He told me before he went from here that he had enough money to grubstake him, and as he wanted to get right away off to some place that these brutes who killed poor old Vicente wouldn't know of, I fancy he was thinking of San Juan."

"Maybe he'll be able to put us on to something if so," said John. "He'll have been there all the early part of this summer. We'll be in luck if we can get a straight tip. But, say, we'd best make a trip first into Santa Fé. We'll get our supplies a lot cheaper there and I'd like a talk with the Agent."

So to Santa Fé we rode, making as straight a shoot as possible across the mesas : we hardly saw a sign of human habitation except the roofs of the Santo Domingo pueblo till we struck the first Mexican houses about seven miles below Santa Fé where the stream sank into the sand and went dry. Here stood up a big public notice and in large capitals at the head of it we read the ominous words, DEAD OR ALIVE, and im-mediately below followed the attractive figures, $3,000 REWARD.

Of course we reined up to see what all this was about. The $3,000 reward was offered for the body (dead or alive !) of a certain outlaw who had held up the stage coach between Santa Fé and Las Vegas on such and such a date. His name was George Hobbes, according to the printed notice, which gave a full description of him as follows : " Smooth face, blue eyes, high colour, long curly hair hanging down on his shoulders ; wears buckskin ; rides with a very long stirrup ; looks like a boy on horseback." And every single point in this description could be applied to me. John read the description carefully through and then ran his eyes over me from top to toe with the twinkle in them I knew so well, and on his lips a queer grin.

" Why, Townshend," he said, " I never knowed before as you was a bad man."

Of course I had to grin back, but the thing was really beyond a joke. The points given did fit me so well that some enterprising gentleman might quietly shoot me out of the saddle without more ado for the sake of those $3,000.

We rode those last seven miles into Santa Fé " with the face on the shoulder," in Spanish phrase, that is to say, keeping the sharpest kind of a look out. And the minute we were in town and had stripped our saddles at the El Paso (was it ?) corral, where we stopped, I fled straight off to the barber's and had those too long locks of mine shorn. That at least did make me one point less like the bad man with the $3,000 set on his head, and then at the corral I met a friend who swore that now I was going to be all right. Nevertheless, I was still a trifle nervous when I sallied out next morning to go round to the three biggest storekeepers in Santa Fé whom I knew, in order to find out the price of flour and coffee and bacon, and so forth. John had to go and hunt up his Indian Agent, so as to fix up about his being able to leave Jemez for a while as we proposed, while I got the supplies. As once before I found I got the best terms from Solomon Stendhal, and I also arranged to get the supplies forwarded from Santa Fé to Jemez in due course, but Jemez was so remote that I was told we should have to wait a bit before they arrived. Meantime John fixed up his business satisfactorily with the Agent.

John and I returned safely to the pueblo, for nobody tried taking a shot at me as George Hobbes, and busied ourselves with our preparations for the journey. One of the best-wearing things in the world is buckskin, and I set my heart upon having a pair of buckskin trousers.

" Look here now," said John. " You go on talking about wanting to wear buckskin the same as our Injun friends here do. What's the matter with you making yourself a pair of buckskin pants out of them two deer-skins we got up in the sierra ? They'd be about right for it."

John was just right, as usual, and so were the skins, while, as for me, ambitious as I was to do everything for myself, I set to work to tan them. I soaked those deer-skins, I scraped them and I rubbed in the squashed brains of the deer to soften them, and after that I worked them supple with my hands—a big job it was, too—always under John's expert advice and supervision. Then I took a pair of old trousers and ripped up the seams, and using their component parts as patterns, I cut the pants out of the buckskins and sewed them together with an awl and a buckskin whang to make them extra strong. One of our Indian friends, Fernandez, happened to come in and find me sewing. He watched my fingers awhile with silent interest. Then he said, " Mi amigo esta cosiendo con un lazo." " My friend is sewing with a lasso."

That was his comment on the thickness of the buckskin string I was using, nor could I say that he wasn't correct. But all the same I got the pants finished, and really proud of myself I was when I put them on for the first time.

Really good I found them too for creeping and crawling over rough ground on our next hunt up in the mountains, on which I wore them. But soon, unfortunately, fresh complications arose : there came on a heavy storm while we were out this time, and the new buckskin pants got very thoroughly drenched. I took them off and dried them, also very thoroughly by the camp fire, but, alas, when dry not only had they shrunk but they proved to be as hard as stove-pipes ; it was hopeless to try to get into them as they were, and I pounded and hammered and suppled them again with grievous labour of my hands, only to find that when at last I did get into them and came in for yet another ducking they dried stiffer and worse out of shape than ever.

"It's no use," said John sympathetically. "You've worked at them pants like a beaver, but I see I didn't give you the right tan. White man's tan isn't much use alongside of Injun tan. Better get old Fernandez or one of 'em to tan them pants for you. They'll know how."

John was right again, sure. I got Fernandez to tackle the pants, and he went out in the woods and gathered some herbs that the Indians knew of, and made a brew of them, and tanned the pants with the brew, and from that they came out a fine rich red, rather darker in tone than a boiled lobster.

When I got them wet once again—for, our supplies being slow in arriving, we had one more hunt—they certainly did not go hard, but they did stretch in rather queer unsuspected ways. One leg was now too tight and had grown considerably too long ; the other leg was loose, but full six inches shorter. But anyhow they would still do well enough for our prospecting trip.

And here I think I may jump on a little and tell what became of them ultimately. When John and I went out on our prospecting journey we worked our way through the wild uninhabited country where the Navajos wandered on the north borders of New Mexico and hoped that at last we had got into Colorado. We hadn't seen a white man since I don't know when, and I happened to be riding alone some way on ahead when I caught sight of a man sitting up on the spring-seat of a wagon behind a span not of broncos but of American horses. He was himself an American, obviously, and American too was the wagon, a three-inch Schuttler from Chicago. I thought of my old Colorado days, and it fairly warmed my heart to see such a thing once more. I loped my mare towards him till I ranged up alongside the wagon and without more ado I started talking. He looked at me, shall I say at my wild figure, with a scarcely concealed curiosity.

" Are we in Colorado now," I began, " and is this the Valley of the Animas ? "

" That's what it is," he answered. And then we fell into a conversation, I explaining how my partner and I had just arrived from New Mexico, and pouring out to him many questions as to the Animas and the other forks of the San Juan river and as to how much prospecting for gold was going on there and with what success ? In short, we had a real good talk, he and I. Of course I was a novelty to him, for, I suppose, John and I were about the first men to reach the San Juan, with a view to prospecting, through the Navajo country. Practically the whole San Juan rush came from Colorado, from the north-east, that is to say, and not from the south.

The more we talked the friendlier the American and I grew, but I could not help noticing that what seemed very like a twinkle came into his eye as he looked again and again at my wild figure. Finally he seemed to be mustering up his courage to say something.

" Stranger," he began cautiously, " I should like to ask you a question."

" Why, certainly," said I. " What is it ? Fire away."

" No offence, stranger, you understand," he added, eyeing that 16-shot Winchester rifle across my saddle with a sort of deprecating glance.

" Why, sure," returned I, " no offence taken here. I'm only too thankful to get a white man to talk to at last. Barring my partner, I haven't set eyes on one in a month of Sundays."

" Wal', stranger," he continued, " allus you understand meaning no offence, what I wants to know is, did you make them 'ar pants yourself ? "

Instinctively my eyes followed his down to those wonderful leg coverings I wore, their weird red colour, their bulging knees, and stiff wrinkles.

"Certainly," I answered. "I did make them myself."

"Wal', stranger," said he, "d'you know, I thought so!"

That night I cut them up into buckskin strings.

CHAPTER IX

OFF FOR THE SAN JUAN

TO go back to the start for our prospecting trip, the supplies we had bought in Santa Fé for it arrived at last, and then in no long time John and I found ourselves off for the San Juan.

We started out three, not two, on that adventure. For there turned up at the pueblo a curious sort of solitary wastrel whom we called Tommy Dodd. He was a youthful American with a kink in his brain ; you might call him indeed half-witted, or perhaps three-quarters witted would be fairer. Anyhow he wasn't quite all there and was just aimlessly drifting around from village to village in ever-hospitable New Mexico. He could cook a bit, which was a useful accomplishment, and hearing we were off to San Juan he promptly wanted to go too. So finding him harmless, John and I settled that we would take him along and let him do the cooking while we looked after the horses and Captain Jinks and the burros or pack-jacks we had bought to carry the supplies we had got from Santa Fé. And of course the prospecting when we got there would be our job.

So we said farewell to the Jemez Indians, who I think had really taken me to their hearts—most assuredly I had become extremely fond of them—and we struck out. We plunged into the Navajo country, passing various camps of theirs and finding them quite amiable. In every camp we found one or more Navajos who had picked up Spanish enough at Bosque Redondo to be able to talk with us pretty well : in fact, a few, though only a very few, were almost as easy to talk with as our Jemez friends. The Navajos and their brother tribe, the Jicarilla Apaches, are said by experts to be migrants from somewhere far away to the north. They had been ordinary hunter tribes, but when they got down to the land where they found rest for the sole of their foot, that is to say as far as New Mexico and Arizona, to use the names given to those parts in later days by the Spanish conquerors, there they planted themselves. What was more, as they now could find no buffalo to hunt, they took a hint from the house-building Montezuma Indians on whose border they found themselves and, like them, grew corn and vegetables as their staff of life. But their language they did not change. The pueblo Indians had a great variety of dialects, but the Navajos stuck firm to their own ancestral tongue, so that they could talk to their pueblo neighbours only in that Indian lingua franca, the sign language. Neither did they take lessons from them in house-building. The Navajos stuck

NAVAJO HORSEMEN

to their ancestral hogans or mud-smeared pole shanties for winter and to their little open brush encampment circles for summer. But when the Spaniards came along and brought in cattle and sheep and horses the Navajos took to them like ducks to water, to the two last especially, and proved splendid riders and sheepmen. Also when the Spanish priests got a hold on the pueblos and made them become at least nominally Christian, they got no such a grip on the nomad Navajos, and the latter naturally stuck to their own religion and remained pagans of a quite unadulterated order. It was, perhaps, as well for our peace of mind that we did not understand the Navajo language, for each of their camps was just then buzzing like a wasps' nest over the news that had come from the North, that the white man had proved no longer invincible, for the Sioux had wiped out Custer and every man of his 260 cavalry. But we knew nothing of all this, and the Navajos we came across seemed none the less friendly. The thing that struck me most among the Navajos was the position of their women : I don't mean that it was actually higher than it was with the Jemez ladies, but compared to the Utes it was absolutely, as John called it, " way up tony." The Ute women that I had seen seemed to be the merest drudges, slaves in fact. Hadn't a Ute warrior offered up there in Colorado to trade me his second-best squaw for the Sharpe's rifle I carried in the days before I got a Winchester.

But these Navajo women paraded around in their camps just as big as anybody and evidently felt themselves to be quite independent, quite all right. Much I wondered at this at the time, but long afterwards I came across a story that might possibly have something to do with their high position. It was a story of the spirit-world, to the entering of which the Navajos, like all Indians, look forward with no small amount of anxiety. Well, in the Navajo spirit-world, before you can attain to the abode of bliss you have to pass a spiritual San Juan whose Styx-like flood quite shuts off ordinary ghosts from Elysium. This San Juan has seven streams, and every one of the seven has awful quicksands, and if you so much as try to get across by yourself you are practically dead sure to sink in them and be lost for ever. But there is one way of salvation and one only, and that is to be friends with Madam Whailahay. She is an old, old Navajo woman who knows the fords and can lead you safe through those awful quicksands into Elysium. But she has one absolute rule : unless you have been good to the Navajo women here on earth she will not help you ; you may find those fords for yourself and take the certain consequences. Is it to be wondered at if Navajo true believers treat their earthly women decently ? I can't swear that this story is the cause of so beneficial a result, but it does look very much as if it might be. I dare say I might have found all this out for myself at the time of our trip instead of waiting for years to happen upon it in a scientific report, but I was then absorbed entirely in the idea of finding gold.

Of course we were still many scores of miles from the gold diggings, but I dreamt of gold every night and each blessed day I strove to work those jacks along towards the gold country as fast as we could get them to go. So we didn't stop long in the Navajo camps, which now that it was summer were pitched high up on the mesas wherever there was any water, and we worked our way down the dry endless Cañon Largo to the San Juan. Water was precious scarce, but we managed the drive somehow, and so we got to the San Juan at last.

We hadn't seen a human being, not for days, for that part of the country was only inhabited by the wandering Indians in winter, and of course there were no whites nor any sign of them anywhere.

Then at last we came out upon the San Juan, the temporal not the spiritual San Juan, and a noble valley it ran through. The river itself I should guess was a good deal bigger than the Thames ; and the low grounds on either side of it which were partly flooded in spring when the snow on the high mountains melted often ran back a good half-mile or more to the foot of the rolling uplands. The grass was splendid, and it was plain to see that by taking out irrigating ditches from the river it would be as good as, ay,

H

even a better country for agriculture than, the Rio Grande. We were most enthusiastic over it, both of us.

"See here," said John. "This is bound all to be a white man's country some day; the Injuns won't be allowed to keep this; and I don't believe it will be so very long neither. Just for the present it's assigned to the Hickories (Jicarilla Apaches) by the Government, but they don't come here hardly ever. They like better to hang around Tierra Amarilla where they can swap off Government rations to the Mexicans for whisky. So now you hear me talk. Let's you and me come back and take up ranches and settle down here when that day comes. It's God's own country, that's what this is."

"Right you are," said I. "I'm good to try it when the time comes. Of course it's not possible now. It's far too soon."

"That's just what I was saying," said John. "The time isn't come yet, but it won't be long a-coming. Maybe another five years will see this a white man's country. So what's the matter with our planting that bag of peach stones I've brought along from Jemez, so we'll have our peach orchard all ready started for us beforehand?"

John had got in the pack a little sack of peach-stones he had procured from good orchards over on the Rio Grande for this very purpose. He had a brain that could look ahead to some purpose. Now he got out that sack and, leaving Tommy

Dodd to cook, he and I wandered along the low grounds and where we saw likely spots, places damp enough to give the seeds a chance to swell and grow but not so exposed to the current as to be in danger of being washed away by floods, there we dibbled those peach-stones carefully in. It was a curious feeling, to look at that glorious valley lying there empty without a sign of human occupation anywhere, and to think that in a few years all would be so utterly and completely changed. Yet that the change would come was as sure as that day follows night or summer winter. Into my mind there came the memory of the verse, " The wilderness shall blossom as the rose." No truer word was ever spoken, and now that man has shown such marvellous powers of triumphing over the difficulties of Nature I should not wonder if the Kalahari Desert itself were yet to be turned into the Garden of Eden.

Of course there was no use prospecting in the actual San Juan River down here far outside the mountains, and accordingly we struck up northwards over the high ground that divided the Los Pinos and the Las Animas forks of the main river till we descended into the broad open park lying quite far up on the Las Animas. We guessed ourselves to be entirely out of New Mexico now and well up into Colorado, and here at last were again the habitations of men.

That first night we camped on the upper Animas there came a storm of rain that fairly flooded our camp, so that we spent most of the next day drying our things. I must anticipate here to say that nigh on thirty years afterwards, when I revisited New Mexico in my old age and found my old partner John happy with a wife and a son living up at Jemez Springs, almost the first word he said to me after helping me down from the post-office vehicle was :

" Townshend, do you remember that first night as we camped on the Animas ? "

" Yes," said I, " not much fear of my forgetting that ! "

" Well," he went on, " d'you know that night we was camped on the richest anthracite mine in Colorado ? "

Yet it wouldn't have been much good to us in 1876 if we had known of it, for coal had not yet got to be an important asset in that remote district. Gold, gold, gold was what all men wanted then.

But gold, that is to say good gold, coarse gold, gold that would pay to wash in a flume, was just what we could not find. Up and down all the side gulches of the upper Animas we panned : John had already taught me how to scoop up a shovelful or two of likely-looking gravel into a pan, then to shake it well round under water in a pool, rake off or toss off boldly the top gravel again and again till only a little was left ; then to throw off more carefully the finer gravel till you could see only the black sand left at the

PANNING FOR GOLD IN A MOUNTAIN STREAM

bottom which was heavy iron ore and remained after the gravel. Then you threw a cupful or so of water round in the angle of the pan, making the black sand streak itself along, and at the tail of it you might spot a bright yellow sparkle. That meant gold. But if it was only yellow specks it was no use: you couldn't save specks in a flume ; you must have coarse gold, in grains as big as shot. Finding specks, of course, meant that there was more gold somewhere in the mountains where the gravel came from : but it was only coarse gold that meant pay-gravel. Almost everywhere we could find the colour, as the specks were called, the much-longed-for coarse gold never. Somewhere or other it must be, but Lord only knew where.

We met a good many other American prospectors in the course of these wanderings ; however, their luck was not one bit better than ours. Then we heard of a lone Mexican who was said to be actually working a claim for gold, though he was reported to be content with a mighty poor return for his work. His diggings were over on another creek. I pricked up my ears at this and deserting John for a couple of days I went over to where they told me he was. As I had suspected, the Mexican was Gus ; all the company he had was a little black dog—Little Dog he called him— which he had picked up somewhere, and right glad did he show himself to see me. Of course we had a great crack together over the camp-fire; I gave him all the latest news of Jemez, and he told me how he had tried for gold in innumerable gulches till he had come to the end of his grubstake, and now here he was working a small claim all by himself with only a couple of short lengths of flume and taking out less than half a man's wages, perhaps some $2 a day. Still he had to buy grub, and even that little would help him a bit both now and for next winter. When I told him how John and I had come up through the Navajo country he was eager to know if we had prospected any down below on the San Juan itself.

"No," I said, "where we were the river was far outside the mountains. The mesas there were all sandstone : it was no use to think of trying for gold." Though I had only just become a gold prospector, already I could talk grandly enough as to where gold ought and ought not to be found.

"Well, now," said Gus, "I tell you something. I knew a Mexican once who bin a captive among the Navajos in the war. And he say they have one cañon there in the San Juan country where they pick up little yellow stones. Now I'm sure they never come up here into these high mountains because of the Utes ; so might his cañon be down somewhere near the San Juan."

"Well, if his story's true," I said, "and if the little yellow stones were gold (which I doubt) what's the matter with this lost cañon of his being somewhere in the country of the Jicarilla Apaches. They are like brothers with the Navajos, so they might go in there and pick up gold (if there was any) and the San Juan comes out of the high mountains somewhere there. If you want to look for this Mexican's lost cañon I guess that'll be the line to strike."

Gus assented to this, and anyway, as he was tired to death of working this wretched little claim of his, he decided promptly on my invitation to pull up stakes and join John and me, as I swore to him that we had lots of grub for all of us. So back to John he and I went, and we all three did our prospecting in common. But there was no turn in our luck, and no coarse gold ever showed up in a single one of the many pans in many gulches that we washed. All the latter part of that summer we did work at prospecting most industriously, but with never a sign of our much-hoped-for reward.

And then a most disgusting thing happened to us. John Miller developed real bad rheumatism in his back, which of course made it absolutely out of the question for him to work : all he could do was to sit round the camp-fire and roast his poor back and perhaps lend Tommy Dodd a hand with the cooking. Knowing he was now nothing but a mere drag upon us naturally made him feel very low in his spirits, and it also made his inward thoughts run back more and more to those snug warm quarters he had left behind in New Mexico there at the pueblo of Jemez.   But we had found a lovely warm rest-camp in one of the side gulches of the Animas, and it was finally decided that John with Tommy Dodd should try what roasting John's back at the fire there might do for him before he chucked it all and fled away to Jemez. Meantime Gus and I would put in a real hard bit of prospecting on the headwaters of the Animas.

CHAPTER X

THE STORY OF THE DUN HORSE

SO leaving John there to roast his lame back Gus and I lit out. Of course Little Dog went with us, and John let us take Keno along too. We left the pack-jacks with him and took just my mare and Jinks and Gus's horse, which was an evil-tempered stallion, a mouse-coloured dun with black stripes of the genuine Mexican plug species. We made our way to the upper valley of the Rio de Las Animas, and we had got into an almost inaccessible cañon where perhaps no white man had ever found his way before. But I had had the luck to discover a concealed trail, once used by the Utes, which led into it through a perfect network of precipices, and when we reached the river's bed, a thousand feet down, and found the gold there running as high as forty "colours" to the pan, we determined to work our way up the bed of that cañon and see if there was more gold where that came from. It was a weird place, the bottom of that cañon. Great mountains too steep to climb rose on either side from the trough through which the river roared, and the pent-up torrent, foaming white over black shining boulders, twisted its way from side to side, like a spotted silver snake trying vainly to climb the dark precipices that walled it in. At every bend of the stream it left a little horseshoe-shaped flat of level ground on the side opposite to where it dashed against the cliffs, and these morsels of dry land were densely wooded with thickets, impassable save by the deer-paths that criss-crossed through them like a maze. Through these thickets, though, we had to hack a way for the laden pack-mule with the axe, only to come out again every time on the cold rushing stream, dangerous with slippery boulders and shifting sand-bars. Then we stopped to wash a pan or two and look eagerly in the bottom of it, at the tail of the " black sand," for the yellow sparkle that lured us on ; and then not finding it rich enough we pushed on across the next bend. Every time we forded that wan water we knew we were plunging one step deeper into a trap, where two days' rain might swell that silver snake into a monster whose strangling embrace meant death. Not lightly was that river named the Rio de Las Animas, the River of Lost Souls.

Reckoning on being able to get back easily to Silverton we had only brought a moderate supply of grub, nevertheless we pushed on till our food almost gave out, but no coarse gold, no gold in the round, heavy nodules and water-worn nuggets that mean a fortune for the discoverer, could we find. Gold there was in all the bars; ay, in every pan we washed, but it was only the light non-paying " flour " and " scale " gold, too poor to work, but tempting you to go on everlastingly in the hope of something better.

Then came down the rain for one night, one only, and the river rose, not enough actually to drown us out, but enough to imprison us for three days on one of the brush-covered flats from which we could move neither up nor down. The horses were all right, for they found plenty of rich mountain grass in the brush, while we drew our belts tighter and looked with hungry eyes on Captain Jinks, the little sorrel mule, who was as fat as a seal. But Jinks was our pet; the best little mule that ever carried a pack; he followed the mare like a dog, not needing to be led; and before we ate Jinks we'd have starved for a week, and then gone a hole tighter to give him a respite. But already we had cut ourselves down to quarter rations, four ounces of flour and four ounces of bacon a day, and as for Keno and Little Dog, their share was small indeed. When we had finished our preposterously minute dough-cake and skimpy rasher of bacon, we put the pan back on the fire, with one spoonful of flour to brown in it, and then poured in a cupful of hot water, and let the mess swell. I can see those dogs now, sitting on each side of the pan, their tails thumping the ground, their lips watering and twitching as they waited till the mess was cool enough to lap. Then we scraped it out on our two tin plates, one for each dog, and if ever platters were licked clean those were.

The Rio de Las Animas flowed from the Pacific slope of the Rocky Mountains, and the flora of that side of the range differs considerably from that of the Atlantic. Many of the wild plants were then actually unnamed and unknown to botanists, and to experiment upon eating unknown fruit is none too safe. There was a tale of two soldiers who had got lost and ate strange fruit up in the sierras, and succeeded in knocking their heels against the backs of their heads in strong convulsions before they died. That gave one to think. At the same time, when you see a bright, wholesome looking red berry close to your mouth, the impulse to pluck and eat is apt to be too strong for the most prudent of us. At least before long I succumbed to temptation and I ate, and then— whether it was conscience, or the red berries, I can't say, but I began to feel, not indeed actual pain, but the uneasiness that makes one feel perfectly sure the pain is coming. In sudden terror I turned to Gus, "Look here," I cried to him, "am I getting green?" He looked, and a grin came over his face. "Huh! you bin eating some of them berries, I know! No, you not green; you not even pale yet. But you go on and eat these queer things what grow in this country and I guess the wolves eat you." But three hours later, when he saw I was still alive, I caught him having a worry at the same berries himself. " Now, look here," said I, " this won't do. If we both get poisoned there won't be any-one left to conduct the funeral. Let's get back out of this hole and make for Silverton. And won't we have a dinner when we get there." " All right," said he, " to-morrow morning, back we go."

To-morrow morning we rolled up the camp out-fit, light enough now all our provisions were gone, and packed it on Jinks. I saddled my mare, but Gus chose to go afoot. He intended to let the evil-tempered dun run loose and follow us with Jinks, who followed like a dog.

We started down the cañon, and forded the first bend of the river. Gus always laughed at me when it came to fording, for I detested it so heartily. Give me a broad open river to swim and I was ready enough, but to stagger and struggle through that icy foaming torrent on the back of a horse whose hoofs slipped on the rolling stones and plunged into unseen holes, and who might fail to recover himself from the next stumble and go down heavily, pinning his rider under him, I could never enjoy that experience ! Now, Gus was no good when it came to swimming, there I had the laugh at him, but he crossed and recrossed that detestable Rio de Las Animas without a shiver. We turned as we reached the strand, and Jinks splashed up after us like a dog, but the dun was not beside him. That gentleman had enjoyed his freedom for several days, and had no mind to follow. However, we went on, trusting he would think better of it, and threaded the mazes of the brushwood and crossed the river once again, but no impatient whinny told that the dun was beginning to feel lonely, not a sign of him was to be seen or heard.

"Look here, Gus," said I, "I'll wait a bit here with the outfit and you go back and fetch him."

I waited and waited till past noon, and Gus did not return. I took the pack off Jinks, not to make our noon meal, for there was no meal to be made, but to give our faithful little beast a rest. At last there was a crashing in the brush and Gus appeared, very tired, very angry, and without the dun !

" I don't know how going to get him," he cried ; " that infernal brute don't let me catch him, and when I try drive him to the water along the trail we made, he break away every time and run off into the brush."

" You couldn't lasso him ? " I asked, for Gus was known to be one of the best ropers in Colorado.

" How I going to lasso him ? " he returned indignantly. " Those willows and brush grow ten feet high right to the water's edge, and as thick as the hair on a dog's back. No man can throw a lasso without he got room to swing his arm."

" Well," said I, " you can't afford to lose him.

We'll picket Jinks here, and you and I'll go back together and see if we can drive him."

Back we went, fording for the third time the many crossings of that wild torrent, till we reached the stronghold of the wily dun. Struggling along deer paths, sometimes leaving my mare, sometimes leading her through the tangled thickets, we endeavoured to circumvent him and drive him before us down to the ford. People talk of a horse laugh! That dun horse laughed, yes, laughed in our very faces! Switched by the willow rods, torn by thorns and tripped up by roots, we had no more chance of catching him than a tortoise had of catching a hare. The shades of evening began to fall, we had been chasing him the best part of the day, and were faint and weak with hunger. "I don't see what you can do, Gus," I cried. "He's got a soft thing on us, in this brush. What do you say? Shall I crease him?"

Creasing a horse is shooting him through the top of the neck so as to temporarily paralyse the beast by grazing the spinal column. An inch too high and you miss him altogether; an inch too low and you kill him dead. I was so angry that I didn't much mind if I did drop him. But the Mexican had a card to play yet.

"Hold on a bit, Capitan," he said. "I know a trick I like to try. You got some string?" I always kept bits of string in my pocket in camp. "You bin' notice," continued Gus, "when we try to head him to the ford that horse always break away down that deer path to the left."

"Yes," I answered. "That's where he has dodged us every time."

"Next time," said the Mexican, "maybe he run into something new in that deer path."

He went up the deer path on foot, carrying his lasso, and tied one end of it to the stoutest young tree he could find in the brush. Then he opened the noose and deftly disposed the loop like a square across the path at the height of a horse's head, tying it lightly with my bits of string to the branches above and on either side. Now for a last try ! I on the mare and Gus afoot, we hunted the brute here and hunted him there, till we once more had him before us heading down to the ford, and once more he swerved away from us and plunged down the deer path. Gus gave a yell, and flung himself into the path on his tracks. The dun dashed on, and the next minute there came a startled snort and a sound of struggling and tearing in the bushes. The lasso was choked tight round his throat, and our fugitive was captured at last.

All this time, the melancholy wails of Jinks, bereft of his beloved mare, who to him was " more than a sister, more than a mother, more than a maiden aunt," resounded through the walls of the cañon, but now his vigil was ended. Gus rode through the ford dragging the reluctant dun by the rope at the horn of his saddle while I vengefully thrashed him with a lariat from behind. It did not take long to reach the place where I had dumped the outfit, repack Jinks and push on down the cañon till darkness stopped us and we lay down supperless to rest. All next day we rode hungry, save for some miserable apologies for potatoes that we found at the bottom of an old sack in an abandoned claim shanty. The day after that we at last emerged from the labyrinth of mountains and cañons and saw below us the little mining town of Silverton.

"Now, Gus," said I, "you go down to the river quick and off saddle and start a fire, and I'll lope into town and be back with grub before you can say 'knife.'"

He turned off the beaten trail at once, and in five minutes, while the butcher was cutting the ten pounds of best tenderloin steak I ordered, and the Jew grocer wrapping up the needful coffee and sugar, I was stuffing a gunny sack full of delicious fresh loaves from the German baker opposite. It was hard to stand in the shop and not take a mouthful, but I felt bound in honour not to taste food before Gus. The fire was burning briskly by the time I got to camp, although I fairly made the mare fly to reach it. Ten pounds of steak. Well, at that dinner we made up for the arrears of a week!

Did we forget Keno and Little Dog? Not much! But they were well ahead of us already.

I

Not a quarter of a mile from where we were camped the Silverton slaughter-house stood on the bank of the river, and the dogs' keen noses had told them what a savoury repast awaited them there. An hour later, as we lay lazily basking in the afternoon sun, enjoying the post-prandial pipe, we laughed consumedly to see those two dogs come waddling back, their sides bulging out so that they could scarcely get along.

As for the dun, we worked him all autumn, and he was as well and as wicked as a horse could be till suddenly one winter's day he died ; we believed out of sheer bad temper, for neither of us could ever discover any other reason for his decease. And yet there was a kind of pathos about his end too. He was grazing one day when we were camped on the San Juan with the mare and the mule. Suddenly he seemed to stagger and reel, and he went up to the mare and tried to put his head against her side, as if asking for sympathy. But animals hate their sick fellows, and she bounded indignantly away from him. Then he raised his head high up, and he turned in the direction of his beloved Mexico that lay far away, as if he knew exactly where it was, and as if he would take one long last look across the weary leagues that separated him from the valley where he was born and from which we had brought him. And then he gave a keen and most pitiful neigh, a neigh such as I never heard a horse give before, and he fell down dead.

No doubt we were right in calling it heart disease ; but we should never have guessed he had a heart if it had not been for that pitiful neigh.

CHAPTER XI

THE LOST CAÑON

FROM Silverton Gus and I made our way as
quick as we could to the rest-camp where
we had left John. Alas, his poor
rheumatic back was no better, and finally the
three of us agreed that the best plan would be
for him to take Tommy Dodd and go right straight
back to Jemez while Gus and I stuck to the prospecting until snow began to fly. Once the frosts
begin you can't do much more work with your
pan in the streams.

But Tommy, as I have indicated, was not a
very efficient sort of person, and in the end we
decided that Gus and I had better leave the pursuit of gold for a bit and personally take poor
crippled John back to Jemez, or at least most of
the way there. We should see how we got on
anyhow.

And so it was fixed : Gus and I packed the jacks
and Captain Jinks, and all four of us started south
by easy stages. By the time we got to the San
Juan John's rheumatics were distinctly better.
Naturally the climate was milder down here : we
were well out of the mountains and I dare say

quite two or three thousand feet lower than where we had been looking for gold. We crossed the San Juan with but little trouble, the river was at its lowest in the fall, and soon found ourselves out among the Navajo sheep camps. The Navajos were as friendly as ever.

"See here now," said John to Gus and me, "there's a good month yet that it'll be possible to go on prospecting back yonder before snow flies. Why don't you and Gus go back for one more last try? The luck might turn: you never can tell."

John was every bit as keen on the chance of getting hold of a gold claim as either of us.

"But how about you?" I queried.

"Oh, I'll do fine," he answered. "My back is much better, and it isn't so far to Jemez now, and if I did feel real bad again I could get some of these Navajos to lend me a hand: they're only too glad to get the chance of earning a dollar."

John, in fact, knew just where he was and what he could do. And so naturally what he said went. Gus and I packed a good lot of our remaining supplies on Captain Jinks, shook hands with John and parted.

"If we do strike anything rich we'll let you know first thing so you can chip in too."

These were my last words to John as Gus and I turned in our saddles and struck back for the mountains once more. The idea of the lost cañon had fastened its grip upon us and we had it in the back of our minds as we prospected up and down many rivers and streams, the various forks of the Las Animas, the Pinos, and the Piedra— we searched them all, and we found " the colour " everywhere, but not the lost cañon. It was most tantalizing. It seemed as if there was gold all around us, only we could not succeed in hitting on the spot where it was plenty.

In September we found ourselves nearly down to the San Juan, not very far below the cañon where the river cuts through the mesas. Finally we crossed the river and had a try in the very unlikely-looking country on the other side. It was in vain. Here Gus climbed a mesa one thousand feet high, and brought back with him from the top of it a handkerchief full of rich-looking gravel. We panned it out in the river, and there was " the colour " again.

" The colour " was everywhere, but where were the coarse gold and the big nuggets ?

Our provisions were now nearly run out. We had only two days' food left. We were sixty miles from Tierra Amarilla, a frontier place in northern New Mexico and the nearest settlement. We decided to go there, buy some food, and come back and try again.

Accordingly we started off, taking the Indian trail through the mesas, made by the trading Navajos going to Tierra Amarilla.

As soon as we left the river the country was

absolutely waterless. The mesas were level or slightly undulating flats, dotted all over with cedar and piñon trees, and with plenty of rich grama-grass growing everywhere. They were intersected by many dry side-cañons, with perpendicular walls of yellow sandstone, all ultimately leading down to the main cañon of the San Juan, which drained the whole country.

Far away through the clear air we could see the vast circle of snowy mountains in which the river had its sources, and from which the gold we were looking for must have originally come.

We had filled our canteens with water in the morning at starting, which gave us enough for our noon camp, and that evening we had the good fortune to find a tiny water-hole in the high and dry mesa we were crossing ; and by it we camped.

The next morning, as we were setting out, looking westward toward the river we saw a broad, smooth, almost level valley.

Gus looked long and earnestly at it.

" That look mighty like the place that Mexican been tell me of," said he, " accordin' to the way he talk about it."

" Well," I answered, " we've got one day's provisions still. The main cañon here can't be more than fifteen miles away in a straight line. Let's have a try to get down to it. We can come back here to-night, and go hungry to-morrow till we get to Tierra Amarilla."

" All right," replied he, and we promptly turned our horses' heads to the left and headed for the river, Jinks following obediently.

The stock were in capital condition, and we pushed them along. At first all went smoothly ; we travelled rapidly down the broad, open valley, which was bordered on each side by low lines of rock.

After a few hours' travel our valley had contracted to a width of a quarter of a mile, and the rock walls were higher, perhaps some twenty or thirty feet ; we were now well below the level of the mesa, and could no longer see out of the valley.

Another hour's travel, descending all the time, and we found our valley becoming distinctly a cañon, one of the side-cañons of the river ; it had closed in so as to be quite narrow, and the sandstone walls were over a hundred feet high.

It no longer ran fairly straight, but zigzagged from side to side, which would make the journey to the river far greater than had seemed to be the case from the above at its head. We travelled on all day, for we hated to turn back without having reached our goal, and we determined to push on. Just before evening we came to a place where the walls opened out somewhat, and there was a beautiful spring of sweet water and plenty of grass. We camped here for the night ; our animals were in clover.

We cooked the last of our food, and settled

that, as the river must now be quite close, we would go down to it quick in the morning, have just one try for luck in it—it is always " just one try "—and then by a hard push reach Tierra Amarilla at latest in thirty-six hours. We would take in our belts a hole, and go hungry for a day and a half.

At daybreak we started on down again, but we did not reach the river so quickly as we had hoped. The side-cañon we were following zigzagged more than ever. The rock walls grew higher and higher.

We seemed to be going down into the very bowels of the earth.

The wilder and more uncanny the place grew, the more certain we felt that the gold was hidden somewhere down here. The cañon wound like a series of S's, and every time we turned a corner we expected to see the river at last, but saw only the interminable walls of our prison. We were near a thousand feet down now.

Suddenly we were brought to a halt. In front of us the bed of the cañon broke away in a steep precipice eight or ten feet down.

We dismounted, and leaving our horses we climbed down. Then we got boulders and pieces of driftwood, for floods ran down the cañon evidently after rain, and with them we built up an inclined plane at the foot of the steep place till our animals were able to jump down in safety.

On again deeper and deeper still the chasm led us. It was a scene of utter barrenness.

Naked rock everywhere, and no sign of life ; no sound ; no breath of air ; a stillness as of death.

Suddenly rounding a bend we heard a roar of waters ahead, we were nearing the San Juan at last. Turning the next corner, we saw it before us, running dark and strong between huge walls of the everlasting yellow sandstone.

Where our side-cañon joined the main gorge the walls at the angle were somewhat broken away, and became less precipitous ; but both above and below the junction the cañon was most forbidding, filled from side to side with the rushing stream.

We had worked so hard to get to this place that we could not help hoping against hope, against all appearances, that it might be the spot.

We seized the pick, pan and shovel from Jink's pack, and not stopping to unsaddle we ran to the water's edge and began to pan. We did not even get " the colour." We tried above, we tried below as far as we could get, but without success.

It was now near nightfall. Fortunately there was a little patch of grass here and a little more room for our camp than we had seen anywhere for miles back in our horrible trap of a cañon, so we made camp.

There was driftwood for fuel ; we boiled our flour-bag, and the flour sticking to it thickened the water into a thin gruel. We boiled our sugar-bag for sweetening, and this was our supper, a scanty one enough.

That was a hungry night. We talked over this horrid place we had come down and wondered how we should get the horses back up over the precipice that had stopped us on our descent.

"Maybe," said Gus, "we might get the horses up on to the mesa here. This place much less steep than any we been see. If we only get up on the flat mesa, then we lope all the way to-morrow to Tierra Amarilla."

So at dawn we climbed up the side on foot, and found that by two hours' work we could build a trail which would be practicable for the horses out of the gorge. Before noon we had them up on the level mesa and said good-bye for ever, as we hoped, to our prison.

We started at once over the smooth expanse for Tierra Amarilla. We were foiled this time, but the lost cañon should yet be found.

At any rate, we were out of that nightmare-like dungeon of a place at last. We breathed a larger air ; our eyes were free to range at will over sixty miles of mesa and mountain.

Our spirits rose and hope revived. Our horses, glad to be on turf again and off the rocks, shared in our cheerfulness and loped gaily ahead.

Suddenly we were brought to a dead stop. A great gulf yawned at our very feet. Right across our course the mesa was cut by another cañon like that which we had descended, not quite so deep, perhaps, but what of that ? A fissure five hundred feet deep, with sides like the walls of a house, is not to be crossed without wings.

We turned to the right to try to head it, and after an hour's travel succeeded in finding a crossing-place where we could with difficulty lead our stock down one side and up the other. The moment we were over, we turned again for Tierra Amarilla, and loped forward once more.

But presently another cañon as forbidding as the last ran through the mesa and we were stopped again. The whole mesa here was a labyrinth of these fissures, and we were getting into a very awkward situation.

"Capitan," said Gus, "this mighty bad luck. These horses had no water since dawn. Our canteens now half-empty. There's no water on these high mesas. Maybe we get lost up here, and then we going to be in a bad fix."

"Well," I asked, "what are we to do?"

"Better we go back," said he; "We get back to-night down to the river again. Grass there and water. Next day we go up that mean cañon again, and then travel all night to Tierra Amarilla. If we get lost up here, we might lose these horses, then we done for."

"That's so," I answered. "Look here, though. My mare is fresh yet. You stay here and give your horse and Jinks a rest, and I'll take a run up to that high point yonder, where this side-cañon seems to head. If I can see any sort of way out of it we'll make a push for it. If I can't then we'll go back to the river and up that horrid cañon again."

I struck the spurs into my California mare—she could go for ever—and I galloped away to the right.

In about three miles I reached the foot of the high point, and here I found was the head of the last cañon, which was now quite shallow and passable, and here, oh, joy! I saw fresh horse tracks.

Springing off and examining them, I made out that they were probably the tracks of two or three Indian ponies travelling in the Tierra Amarilla direction. I knew that the Indians knew every foot of the country, and of course, like other men, Indians must drink. Their trail would lead to water somewhere. It was practically certain that these Indians would prove to be Navajos, and the Navajos with the memories of Bosque Redondo still fresh in their minds were very much on their best behaviour. There would be little or no danger if we fell in with them.

Back to Gus I loped with a lightened heart, and told him what I had seen. He quickly saddled, and we were soon at the spot. He agreed that the trail was that of Indians travelling, and we decided to follow it. It was marvellous how it led us through that labyrinthine maze of cañons and mesas. But still no water appeared.

Then night came on us and we could no longer see to follow the trail. We made a dry camp and comforted ourselves as best we could by smoking and warming ourselves at a fire of crackling cedarwood. We took it by turns to watch the stock, fearful lest thirst should make them break loose and leave us afoot.

But hunger kept us both awake. A night like that seems an age.

At last came the welcome morning star in the east, and then the gray dawn. We saddled up and, shivering and weak, rode forward again on the trail, vainly looking for water.

Suddenly the trail stopped; we had reached an expanse of bare rock where no footmark could be traced. We rode hesitatingly on to it, looking carefully from side to side.

" Agua! agua! " cried Gus. " Here's the water ! "

In the bare rock was a great hole, like a swimming bath, full of clear, cool, fresh water. It was a godsend to us. We and our thirsty beasts drank again and again.

Then we offsaddled, took the horses back a bit to where there was good grass, so that they might feed; feed for us there was none, but we lay there by the water, hungry and tired, consoling ourselves with a pipe. Of a sudden there appeared from somewhere in the rocks a huge brown spider, a tarantula, who walked very deliberately, taking no notice whatever of us, down to the water and along its edge. I could not swear whether he drank out of the hole or not. Possibly the tarantula is a kind of insect that doesn't drink, anyway if a science man says so I can't contradict him. All I know is that he wandered round by the water, looking for food it might be, being hungry like ourselves perhaps. But whatever it was that he wanted down there by the water Gus and I never found out, for something quite different happened. There were a lot of steep, high, yellow sandstone rocks rising out of the mesa a quarter of a mile or so off, and in among these rocks we made out a black point watching us ; it was the head of an Indian ; he took an uncommonly good look at us, but he seemed satisfied with what he saw, for he presently emerged from the rocks and walked towards us, leading a horse by a rope. He was a Navajo clad in a striped blanket. We made the sign of friendship and called out to him, " Amigos, amigos ! "

He came up close and watered his horse, just as we had done, watching us of course all the time, not ostentatiously but with care. You've got to be careful out on the Ragged Edge.

We tried talking to him in Spanish, slow and clear. He seemed fairly able to follow. We told him we were making for Tierra Amarilla. He pointed out the line with his hand. We asked what he was doing. He answered:

" Hunting deer with another Navajo," holding up a finger to indicate only one.

" Have you killed any ? " we asked eagerly.

" Yes, we have got a buck, a big one."

"Will you sell meat?"

"Yes, we will."

Quickly I produced a dollar and demanded meat.

The Indian jumped on his horse bareback and rode off after it, and meanwhile we gathered sticks and made a good fire. He was soon back with a bundle of thin strips of half-dried venison which they had been "jerking." I seized a piece and threw it on the coals to broil.

"You going to eat that meat like that?" said Gus, who was carefully picking out some of the thickest strips.

"Yes," said I, "of course; it's the quickest way to do it."

"You think them Indians been wash their hands before they cut that meat?" he asked.

"Well, no," I said, "I don't suppose they did."

"And you like eat meat after Indians' hands not washed?" said he; and off he went to the pool and slopped and soused, and washed and rinsed his meat well before he would broil and eat it, though it was our third day of hunger. For very shame I had to do the like.

"Gus," said a man to me once who knew him well, "ought to be king among the Mexicans. He's high toned."

CHAPTER XII

A WOMAN WHO WAS

"LOOK here," said Gus after we had filled ourselves up good on the broiled venison of the two Navajos, "I bin take a good look at this country ahead of us. Seems to me if we work south a bit first we get out of these high mesas and deep cañons into more open country: then we strike out east and make Tierra Amarilla."

Gus was a rare good sort of a pathfinder and I agreed. So we left that waterhole of the tarantula and struck south into the lower country, and we did find our way out of that labyrinth of deep dry cañons. Next day we were in country where the Navajos had many camps and sheep herds grazing, and now as we had rather hurried through our purchased venison our souls lusted after fresh mutton. The obvious thing to do was to buy a sheep to kill, and we tried several Navajo camps to see if they would sell us one, but all in vain; we found not a single Indian, male or female, in any of them who could speak even enough Spanish to make a bargain. However, at the last camp where we stopped to inquire a woman managed to make us understand by means of a great many signs, eked out with a few broken words, that beyond the next hill we should find some one who really could speak our language (I say our, for Spanish was now a familiar tongue to me), and who would aid us in buying a sheep.

So on we pushed, and, sure enough, beyond the hill we came upon a solitary Indian camp ; we could see nothing in it, however, but a lone squaw and a couple of Indian babies. It looked exactly like any other of the many Navajo summer camps we had seen ; a little sort of pen, open to the sky, made of a few cut bushes, inside of which on the bare ground lay some rude earthen vessels for holding water and for cooking, together with a bag of corn meal ; and for furniture there was a roll of the famous hand-wove Navajo blankets. That was absolutely all. The Indian man who owned this rancheria was off out of sight, doubtless somewhat close around pasturing his herd of sheep ; and this little pen was his home, or at least it was as much of a home as he wanted or was ever likely to want. The Navajo is a born nomad, the true Bedouin of the New World. We reined up our steeds at the side of the primitive home ; and, seeing no one else, Gus, speaking in Spanish, addressed the solitary woman, and said that we had come because we had been told that we should find there somebody who understood our language, and with whom we could deal.

The woman never looked him in the face, but silently shook her head, and bent down over her cooking pots by her little fire, without answering a word. To the eye she was simply a Navajo squaw, and I was inclined to think that she was only one more of those wild daughters of the desert to whom any other tongue than the gutturals of the untutored Indian was utterly unknown. But I was wrong : she had understood, understood every syllable, and what was more, Gus had divined as much, for I saw him sitting there on his horse, twisting his thick moustache and eyeing her with a look, half pitiful, half amused.

"Come, amiga," he said coaxingly, "come, don't be so shy. It is very clever of you to be able to understand our tongue so well, and I doubt not that you are clever enough to speak it perfectly too."

But for answer she only shook her head again, hiding her face from him, as one ashamed.

Gus, however, was a man not easily baffled ; he had a tongue, too, that few women could resist. He flattered her, he entreated her, he reproached her, always of course in Spanish, till she could bear it no longer. She sprang up quickly, holding her child to her breast, and turned on him with a defiant air.

"Yes," she said, with perfect fluency and perfect accent, "Yes, I do speak Spanish. Now, what do you want here ? "

Gus smiled. He had penetrated her little disguise at any rate.

"Oh, nothing much," he said. "We only called about a little matter of business. But tell me, amiga, first of all ('amiga' is like saying 'my good woman.' It is the way the superior race addresses the inferior), tell me how comes it that you are able to speak our language like one who is purely Mexican?"

"I was of the captives," she answered simply.

"Ah!" he ejaculated, "at the Bosque Redondo."

"Oh, no," she corrected him. "At the Bosque they had only the ignorant savage Indians who surrendered after the war. I was not of the savages. I was a captive long before that, taken when I was a little tiny girl, and I was brought up as a Christian, a handmaid in a great house of the Mexicans."

During the long struggle between the Mexicans and the Navajos, it was common enough for children to be captured in this way, and brought up as house slaves—very much petted slaves, too, sometimes, by their captors.

There was silence for a little space as we sat there in our saddles, and looked down on this woman living out here in the wilderness, with not even a roof to cover her head. She did not appear to suffer in the slightest from actual want. She was brown and healthy, young and well favoured. Yet, behind the look of defiance on her face there seemed to be something appealing in her eyes, something that claimed a spiritual kinship with us, Navajo squaw though she stood confessed.

" And in what house were you brought up ? " asked Gus at last.

" In the house of the Chavez, at Socorro," she replied.

" And the Chavez baptized you and brought you up as a Socorreña—as a Mexican girl of Socorro—I suppose ? " he continued, inquiringly.

" Yes, I grew up so," was her answer.

" But how do you come to be here then ? " he persisted.

" They brought me," she said, and hesitated and then went on. " You know, three years ago, when the Navajos had settled down again in this their own country here, they petitioned the American Government to let them take back all their captives that were living among the Mexicans. They said that they had restored the Mexicans they had held in captivity, and now it was only fair that the Mexicans should give back the Navajo captives that they held. And the American Government listened to them, and said that it was a reasonable thing, and gave them a paper to require that the captives should be given up. And then the great chief, Manuelito, and the other chiefs rode about everywhere along the Rio Grande, and in all the settlements, and showed the paper, and took away all the captives that they found wherever they were. And me they took away also."

"And the Mexicans did not make any resistance?" queried Gus, who being from Old Mexico knew little or nothing of this.

"How could they?" she returned. "Manuelito had the paper of the American Government."

"But if the captives were married," said Gus, "how then?"

"Oh, then the paper allowed that they were not to be taken," she said, and she dropped her eyes, and a little sigh escaped her. The sigh was not lost on the quick intelligence of the Mexican.

"But I think you left your heart there?" he said gently. "Is it not so? And how came it that a handsome girl like you was not married?"

It was inquisitive of him to press her thus, no doubt, but then the whole situation was so unusual. Her reserve had gone now, and the sweet soft sounds of the Spanish tongue, unheard by her for three long years, unlocked her heart. Tears stood in her eyes. "I was not married," she said, with simple frankness. "I was with Don Fulano de Tal (that was not his name, but it will do as well as another). He had a wife living, and we could not be married." The Mexicans, be it remembered, are Catholics, and do not admit of divorce.

"I see. And he did not protect you?" said Gus, gritting his teeth.

"How was it possible?" she answered, deprecating his swift indignation. She would still defend the man who had once been her lover. "How could he do anything? Manuelito had the paper of the American Government."

At this moment a little flock of sheep appeared over the hill; a tall, fine-looking Navajo man was driving them.

"And that Indian yonder is your husband now?" said Gus, indicating with a gesture the shepherd; she answered in the affirmative, with a constrained nod. "And you like him? He is good to you?"

She shrugged her shoulders with a slight air of contempt as though betraying a certain shame at being linked to one below her.

"Oh, but yes," she conceded "he is a good man—for an Indian." But there was a world of meaning in the pause before those last words.

"But he is of your own people," the Mexican ventured. "You are a Navajosa. You are happy with your own people?"

She turned a quick look on us both, the look of an unreconciled rebel against Fate.

"Son salvajes," she said abruptly, "they are savages."

She had the instincts of a civilized woman, and there was something about her own people that revolted her.

" Let us be gone," whispered I quickly to Gus in English. " Meat from this Indian's herd would stick in my throat. Talking to us only makes her more sad, and for her trouble there is no remedy."

She was crying silently now. There was nothing in the world we could do for her, and our presence did but revive the memories that rent her heart. We raised our bridle reins and turned away.

" Don Fulano de Tal was a dastardly hound," hissed Gus to me through his clenched teeth. Then he swung himself round in his saddle with a deep ceremonious bow, and doffed his sombrero. " Dios sea contigo, señora," he cried. (" God be with you, madam.") It was the farewell salute of a caballero to a lady. Was not she a baptized Christian, and her speech the speech of old Castile ?

And there, near fifty years ago, she stood a houseless dweller in the wilderness, where the glorious September sun poured down upon the wide untilled pasturelands of the Navajos, clasping her Indian baby to her breast, while the tears ran down her face at the thought of what she had been and what she was.

I have never been back among the Navajos since, but I have often wondered whether she ever became reconciled. Perhaps the baby helped her.

And I am sure that the American Government had acted throughout with the very best possible intentions. Only we know that they can end by becoming the pavement of hell.

CHAPTER XIII

CAPTAIN PFEIFFER

FROM the Navajo sheep camps we found our way to Tierra Amarilla, and there we found Tommy Burns, a frontier store-keeper, and a good man too, of his sort, but there was another man in Tierra Amarilla who interested us much more than Tommy Burns.

This was Captain Pfeiffer, who, as I gathered, was there as the Government Agent for the Southern Utes, or at any rate for some band of the Utes. Captain Pfeiffer was a Dutchman, not a German but a real Dutchman from Holland, and he had been promoted captain in the U.S. Army for good service during the war, the great war between North and South. Pfeiffer had married a Mexican ; I think she was sister to Kit Carson's wife, so that he was brother-in-law to the great frontiersman hero as well as his brother-in-arms. Of course, Kit Carson had been dead for some time now, and Pfeiffer, a widower, was living with his one son here at Tierra Amarilla. He was just as brave a man as they make 'em.

" He's got scars all over if you ever see him stripped," said Tommy Burns, telling us about

137

him. " That's from his big fight with the Navajo. You see he'd been out with a patrol in the Navajo war, and they hadn't found any Navajos. And, they came to a fine waterhole, and they hadn't had a good wash for a long time. Now, Pfeiffer had his wife along with him : the Holland Dutch are about the cleanest people out and he felt that they did badly want a wash. So he sent his patrol—they was Mexicans—off into the brush, and he and his wife took off their clothes and got into the waterhole to have a real fine old wash. But the Navajos were watching them all the time, and the patrol being some way off, up rushed a bunch of Navajos just on the dead run and loosed off at Pfeiffer and his missus there in the waterhole. They killed Mrs. Pfeiffer plump dead, and a fourteen-year-old Navajo boy who had a bow shot an arrow into Pfeiffer right through his liver.

" Then came the patrol in a hurry, loping up to take a hand soon as ever they heard the shots, and so the Navajos just simply scooted ! The patrol buried poor Mrs. Pfeiffer, it was all they could do, but they took the boy's arrow out of Pfeiffer's liver and carried him back to camp and the doctor fixed him up so as he got well. He's tough as a pine knot, Pfeiffer is. Well, after that, Pfeiffer had an extra-double-down on Navajos. He fought them as long as Government went on making war until the whole Navajo nation almost surrendered ; after that Pfeiffer declined to quit, so he just joined the Utes and fought the remaining Navajos, who hadn't surrendered with the main lot.

"One time he was out with a bunch of Utes, and they was hid in brush watching a big band of Navajos not a great ways off. 'Come on,' says Pfeiffer, 'let's go at 'em.' 'No,' says the Ute chief, 'they're too many for that. We'll wait for 'em here and take 'em on in the brush if they feel like trying it, but not out there in the open.' Well he knew the Utes are better in brush.

"Of course what the Ute chief said went; it was his band of Utes; but that didn't satisfy Pfeiffer. When he found the Utes weren't on for a fight he goes to the edge of the brush and halloes to the Navajos, 'If any man of you wants to fight I'll meet him half-way and we'll have a scrap just the two of us.' 'Nothing doing,' the Navajos shouts back, 'you've got too good guns.' 'Look at here,' says Pfeiffer, 'I'll come naked with nothing but a knife and meet him if so be he'll do the same.'

"One of the Navajo chiefs said he would chip in, so they fixed it like that, and the two men, stripped stark naked, met half-way between the two crowds wearing nothing but a knife apiece, and came to grips. They carved well enough both of 'em, but Pfeiffer let the life out of the Navajo, while the Navajo only wounded him pretty bad. Then the Utes came out of the brush and carried back their man Pfeiffer into it, and there they bound him up and he got well, while the Navajos just simply planted their dead warrior. But that'll show you the kind of a man Pfeiffer is."

We did admire the old hero after that, and we talked to him all we could. He was precious fond of a drop of whisky, and he talked to us all the better after it too. We told him the story of our search for gold in the San Juan country.

"Yes, that's all right now," said he (I don't attempt to reproduce his Dutch accent), "but when there was a rush of American prospectors in there in 1863 the United States Government sent Kit Carson and me to turn them out. The Government had their own hands rather more than full with Johnny Reb just then and they didn't want a Ute war on top as an extra. But the Utes were quite determined to make a war if the prospectors didn't quit their mountains, so Kit and me had to sail in and make 'em go. The prospectors went too : they quite saw that the Government had to do it, and they didn't seem to bear any grudge against us. I remember one day there Kit and I came on a lone prospector —I think he was the last of them to go—washing for gold right there on the San Juan itself. And Kit spoke up and just told him how it was and explained things. And the man quite tumbled to it and didn't talk back or make any fuss. 'Only,' says he, 'it's the very biggest sort of a pity : jes' look in that pan', and he held up to us that last pan he'd just washed, and there we could see the gold at the bottom shining yellow in among the black sand."

"Might he be put it there himself," said Gus. "Men do do such things sometimes."

"No, no," cut in Pfeiffer. "We'd have seen him if he'd done that. That was gold right straight out of the San Juan River."

"Couldn't you take us back there now?" said Gus. "There's no war now. Why couldn't you do that?"

"Well, I dunno but I might," said old Pfeiffer. "Still it's pretty hard to find your way back to a place like that in the mountains which you've only seen once several years ago."

Nevertheless the old hero hardened his heart —he had taken a fancy to Gus and me—and he got on his horse and went out with us for a prospecting trip to find that place on the San Juan where he saw the American miner wash that last pan with the gold in it.

Of course we never found it : Pfeiffer was a perfectly hopeless guide, and he had no more idea of ever finding his way anywhere than the merest baby. Tommy Burns told us afterwards that they never dared trust him out of sight of Camp without a Mexican or an Indian to bring him home. If they neglected to do that he was dead sure to turn up missing.

This was God's truth too, as we found out. He was just a war-dog, the fighting man pure and simple, nothing else. Nor did he care a great deal for gold. Of course he'd have liked to get some just the same as anybody else, but he could do without it all right. Government paid him enough to live on, he liked his Mexicans at Tierra Amarilla well enough, and he liked his friends the Utes better still. He had to get back to meet them, so he said, when they came in for their autumn visit anyway, so we chucked our hopeless search and brought him back to Tierra Amarilla.

Gus and I talked it over. In spite of the old hero being such an utter failure as a guide, we really did believe he actually had seen what he said he had seen, namely a pan washed in the San Juan itself with good gold at the bottom of it. Yes, we would have one more look, late as the season was getting.

A fresh lot of flour, coffee and bacon was packed on Jinks and away we went. We tried higher up the San Juan now, quite far up into Colorado, only we really hardly knew we were there, the country was so wild and unmapped. We got to Pagosa Springs, and right there at last fortune seemed to smile : we found gold, yes, coarse gold, in the San Juan itself just close to the Springs. Could this be old Pfeiffer's lost place ?

" No," said Gus. " He gets lost, but he'd have remembered if these Springs had been close there where he saw that man. But I guess this is good enough for us if there's much more of it."

The trouble was we couldn't find out how much more there was, for down came the frost and it was no longer possible to work.

"Look at here," said Gus. "Let's go out and tell John Miller and get supplies. Then we'll come back here and stay all winter so we can begin right quick in the spring soon as frost goes. And if John's well he can come and join us then, and we'll all have a good thing. With his rheumatics he'll be better off at Jemez this winter."

"Right you are," said I. "The shortest way to get to John is to cut out going to Tierra Amarilla and travel straight back down to Jemez. It'll give us a chance to see our old friends there anyway."

"And our old enemies too," growled Gus. "You hear me talk. Best thing for us to do is to strike straight for Tierra Amarilla. We'll tell old Pfeiffer of course we've found gold, though it's not his lost place, but he can come and join us in the spring if he likes. We'll not get our supplies at Tierra Amarilla but go right on into Santa Fé where things don't cost half as much, and you can write from there to John Miller and he can chip in next spring same as Pfeiffer if he wants to. Then we'll come right back to here with lots of grub for all winter and be able to start in soon as frost goes."

Gus's head was level as usual and we decided to carry out his plan.

I cannot admit that there is anything sordid

in the thirst for gold that lures men into the wilderness. He is not sordid who to win corn drives his furrows over the face of Nature, nor is the hunter a criminal who slays her children in the wild. And in your search for gold, you yourself are but a part of Nature, and when you take from her you do but come into your own.

No, the sordidness, if there be any, is not in the search for gold, but in yourself, in your own motives. And ours I hold were not ignoble. I was thirty, and for seven adventurous years I had led a half-savage life on the frontier. I longed to return to civilization, at least for a spell, to taste once more of art, and books, and society, and to see again with eyes whose focus had been altered by that wild life what the thing called civilization stood for. But for such return the first need was money, and therefore I sought for gold.

With Leonardo it was different. In his own country he had loved a woman; but trouble had come between them—his the fault, as he freely admitted—and, idlest of atonements, he ruined himself by gambling. Worse, he recklessly involved himself in that murder-game Mexicans call politics, and now should he return his life was forfeit to the sleepless vengeance of the winning party.

So we both of us needed gold, gold that should give him a fresh start in a new land and throw open to me the path back to civilization.

Away we went for Tierra Amarilla : but when we got there we didn't much want to stop. The place was simply full of Jicarilla Apaches : they had drawn their rations, and there they were serenading around town like lively fiends. They had got their skins full of Tommy Burns's whisky through the medium of their Mexican friends and were feeling gay. Consequently Gus and I simply went to old Pfeiffer's house and let him know our plans ; then we bought some bread and beef from a Mexican we knew, pretty tough beef it was too, and though it was already dusk we lit out again down the Chama valley to find a camp where we would be well out of the way of those drunken Jicarillas. We had a good bit of a way to go too, for all the grass had been fed off as bare as the back of your hand anywhere near Tierra Amarilla and we pushed on a good couple of leagues before we turned off from the trail into the pine timber.

Dark though it was, we hadn't blundered far before we stumbled on to the prettiest little camping place that two tired men need want to see, good grass for the horses, plenty of dry wood lying about for our fire, and the tall pines to shelter us and to sing us to sleep with the murmuring voice of the wind in their branches. Conveniently near the trail it was too, so that we could start out bright and early in the morning ; and we thankfully stripped off our saddles and Gus picketed the horses while I made a fire and chip-

L

chopped slices of the tough meat on a log à la Texas Tom. The coffee soon was boiled, and our mouths were watering for the fried collops which were nearly done when we heard an unearthly yell down the trail. "What's that mean?" said I, looking at Gus. We listened, and the sound was borne to our ears again on the night wind, and this time it seemed nearer than before. "That them Jicarilla Apaches," said Gus; "and they yell because they mad drunk." Again the horrible chorus rang out, now only some half a mile distant. Gus looked at me in the firelight. "They going to pass pretty close by us on the trail," he said. "They bound to see this fire. They come to see what we do. You know how they boss round among them wretched peons in Tierra Amarilla and order them about like dogs. 'Indian hungry; go cook meat. Indian thirsty: go, make coffee; give sugar, heap sugar. Then they slap them peons' faces if they don't obey. You want to stand that?—or what you want to do?"

"See them in Hades first," returned I hotly.

"Then better we put out this fire," said Gus.

And with that we sprang at the fire and kicked the embers right and left and trampled them all out we could. We shoved the coffee pot and pan under a bush, and grabbed our Winchesters and flung ourselves down behind the log on which I had been chip-chopping the steak. Nearer and nearer came the yells: there were a few live coals still glowing, but the breath of the night wind caused them to glow fitfully. Would the Indians see them as they rode by? They were almost abreast of us now, and the air was a-quiver with their resonant fiendish voices.

I have said that our camp was conveniently near the trail; it seemed rather too near to be pleasant just then! We held our breath and listened. We could see nothing, but there was much comfort in the feel of a Winchester with fifteen shots in the magazine as those yells rang in our ears. Was that a step? That crash in the bush must be an Indian pony trampling its way to us! No, those shouts were farther off. Could they really have missed seeing those tell-tale embers of our fire? Were they really passing by? Yes, they sounded now distinctly farther down the trail. We breathed again more freely. Slowly the harsh voices grew fainter; they sounded fitfully farther and farther off, and the sough of the pine branches came plainer to our ears as the peaceful silence gathered round us once more.

With lightened hearts we jumped up from behind our logs; we heaped together the scattered embers and piled fresh wood on them, and presently the coffee pot began to sing again and the collops were spluttering in the pan, and Gus and I got our square meal at last.

But we were destined to meet with those Jicarillas again! A fortnight later we were

returning by the same trail from Santa Fé, and
almost at this very same spot we met them ;
but they were not drunk this time. Swiftly
and silently they pushed past us. Anxiety,
anger, ay, and fear were visible in their haste.
Some were on horse and some on foot, but three
of them were swathed mummy-like in bandages
and lashed to cross-sticks fastened across a pair
of lodge poles, making rude sledges or " travaux,"
as they were called by the French voyageurs,
the upper ends being tied to the ponies'
backs, while the lower ends bumped along the
ground. Every step the ponies took must have
been agony to the wounded men, who lay there
grim and silent, and their ashen-grey faces turned
with stoical indifference to me as they were dragged
rapidly past.

The Jicarilla band at this moment looked
like hunted wolves, and hunted, indeed, they
were, hunted fugitives, seeking safety in their
mountain fastnesses. They had been drinking
in Tierra Amarilla again, and this last time they
had met their match and something over. It so
happened that a band of Utes had come in there
also to trade, and had started gambling with the
Jicarillas. And between the whisky and the
gambling they started a quarrel, and then out
flashed the knives. The Jicarillas managed to
cut one Ute's throat beyond the power of bandages
to mend, and the Utes on their side had carved
three of the Apaches badly, and these three

unfortunates, cruelly wounded as they were, were being dragged away like this to save, if possible, their scalps. For the Ute braves were bound to have a life for a life. And I looked at the ashen-grey faces of those three wounded red men as they bumped along past me in the trail, and felt that their end was near. Poor wretches, they too were doomed to be numbered among the victims of the drink-fiend, the worst enemy of their race.

CHAPTER XIV

THE ADDLED EGG

SO there we were, off to Pagosa to sit on what we hoped would prove a fortune for both of us just as soon as ever the frost should release its icy grip on the ground and give us a chance to prove what we had got. A good five months or more that would be too, for the Colorado winter is a winter and no error. Forty degrees below zero is the freezing point of mercury; I never owned a thermometer all the time I was out in Colorado, but men swore to me that the mercury froze every winter and well could I believe it. All the same I can remember my feelings as a Coloradan being very much hurt one December when I was living by myself on the ranch after I had got quit of Lew Howell. A blizzard came on to blow, and a stray Texas cowboy was lucky enough to reach the shelter of my cabin where he was able to put his horse into the stable and warm himself over my fire. Then he and I had a good long crack together over cattle and the good prices they were fetching in Colorado.

"Why don't you pull up stakes and take up a

ranch for yourself here ? " said I, " You'll find it would pay you."

The Texan looked at me with a queer grin. " Blank blank," (I dare not quote him literally) " blank blank a country," said he savagely, " where it's nine months winter and three months very late in the fall."

He was severe, but I have to admit that he had an element of truth in what he said. Of course in Colorado 1,000 miles from the sea you get such dry air and such glorious sunshine that you don't suffer as you would otherwise, but the thermometer does go down. And up in the mountains anywhere from seven to ten thousand feet above sea-level the frosts are harder than ever, though the forests do give some shelter from the blizzards. Gus and I had good blankets and a big buffalo robe—it lies on my wife's sofa now —and also we had a little shelter tent ; the tent was no good against cold it was so thin, though it would do to keep off rain in summer. But as the cold increased at Pagosa we cut pine boughs and built a shelter, a sort of conical brush-tent in shape rather like a Navajo hogan. The biting wind, however, worked its way in through the interstices of the boughs and the only remedy we could think of was to cut more boughs. They kept the snow out right enough, but that cruel wind still worked its way through, and we went on piling up more and more boughs till we had for our shelter an untidy cone of them as high as a haystack : had some real old frontiersman happened to see it how he would have laughed.

Of course we could have all the firewood we wanted for the cutting and we mostly kept up a right good fire whether for cooking or for warmth.

Our stock, too, did not do so badly. We fixed a shelter for them among the trees with pine poles and brush which broke the wind for them and kept off the snow when it was storming, much as the hogan did for us. And as there were lots of steep hills all about they found places even when the snow was bad where they could get at the grass on the slopes and so kept themselves going, and as a matter of fact they came out looking well in spring.

Lonely indeed it was for us that winter. There were no prospectors, I fancy, nearer than the Rio de Las Animas or, perhaps, the Rio La Plata many miles away ; no Utes ever showed up, it wasn't a good country for deer in winter, though I managed to get two or three, and the Utes wanted to be where the deer were. It was much too far up in the mountains for the Navajos, so as a matter of fact we had no neighbours whatever. I can't remember now anyone turning up before spring. There may have been a trapper or two wandering about in the mountains setting his traps and taking anything worth taking that he could find in the way of furs, but if there was none came anigh us. But alas, we did have bad luck, or at least one of us did, namely Little Dog, for he came across a bait left by one of these trapping wanderers of the wild. Little Dog, who slept in our blankets and was our great pet, picked up the strychnine bait which some man had put out for wolves. No one could say how long it was since the bait had been put out, but the hateful poison had not lost its venom. We had been out looking after the horses when Little Dog found it and the first we knew he was down with one of those awful convulsion fits. Gus snatched him up in his arms and quickly carried him into camp, but there was nothing we could do ; we had no remedies, no antidotes, and indeed I don't believe there are any for a full dose of strychnine : the only chance is to vomit it up and we had no sort of emetic. Poor Gus : we both loved Little Dog, but he more especially. There by the fire he walked up and down with the poor little dying animal in his arms, and, strong man though he was, he cried like a woman, like a mother over her child, as he hugged and caressed his pet. It was pathetic there in the cold and snow, so lonely and far from any possible aid, to see him wailing over the cruel fate that robbed us of our one object of affection by so painful a death. It was all over at last, Gus took one of our few blankets to wrap the poor little body in, and we made a hole in the frozen ground with the pick and planted it safe from the jaws of any prowling wolf, and missed our companion at every meal all the rest of that bitter winter.

The winter came to an end at last ; higher every day stood the noon sun in the heaven and his life-giving beams warmed the air and thawed the frostbound soil. Even when melted the water was still most bitter cold, but what did that matter to men who were after gold ? The all-necessary water was fluid not solid, and unfrozen was the gravel in the pan. Now we could wash a pan again.

And wash we did : and cruel, too cruel was our disappointment. There, where we had got the coarse gold last fall, not another grain of it could we find, only the bare colour, the wretched little infinitesimal specks you could get almost any-where in every one of the rivers that came from the San Juan Mountains. We tried above, we tried below, we sank prospect holes in the soil of the first bottom, we tried everywhere we could think of and not a sign not a vestige of pay-gravel, of heavy gold, could we get. Our claim was a duffer ; we had sat all that winter on an addled egg. We could not quite give it up yet. We tried up and down all the near forks and gulches, but equally in vain. And then the idea dawned on us that possibly some man who had an idea of getting hold of Pagosa Springs had salted that spot, where we had first tried and found the coarse gold, so that he might claim it as a mining right and include the Springs. Maybe so, but if he had done so he had chucked it afterwards, for he had put no notices up ; had done nothing in fact,—the place, if it ever were a claim, had been chucked.

And now there was nothing for us to do but to chuck it too. Sadly we thought of that lone cold winter all by ourselves with none too much grub, seven thousand feet up, and not a soul to speak to, when we might have been so warm and snug and sociable somewhere well down on the lower Rio Grande in New Mexico instead. But it was too late for that.

All right, then, chuck it we would and did. We settled to go out to Tierra Amarilla, tell Captain Pfeiffer that the claim he had tried to direct us to was no go, write the same to John Miller at Jemez, get fresh supplies at Tommy Burns's store, and then we would see what we would see. Should we put in another summer prospecting or try something else ? All this we talked over during our melancholy ride back to Tierra Amarilla, and there we told our news to Pfeiffer and wrote it to John as we had arranged.

But we found something at Tierra Amarilla that did materially affect our plans. Letters for Gus there were none, poor lone man, but for me there was a budget both from home and from Colorado Springs. The letters from home had no bad news, but they did make me feel homesick. It was eight years now since I had seen my people, and I did eagerly wish for a sight of them again. And the letters from Colorado Springs made the idea quite practicable. Part of the purchase money of my ranch and cattle had been duly paid and the rest, due next year, seemed perfectly safe. If I did go home my interests out here would be all right, and I could decide later whether to go on trying my luck on the Ragged Edge or have a shot in some other part of the globe. Yes, I made up my mind I would strike for home.

But what about Gus ? He, poor chap, had no home to strike for, and the part of New Mexico where we had friends was much too hazardous for him on account of the hostility of Vicente's murderers. Also wages were much lower in New Mexico than Colorado. We talked it all over, and he decided to accompany me back to Colorado Springs : he was always worth $40 to $50 a month there, where he was so well known as an A1 cowboy, and he always got on well with Americans. It ended by our starting back for the Springs.

I got a cordial good-bye from Pfeiffer, the old hero whom I honoured, and I wrote a long fare-well to John Miller, to whom I could not get near enough for a handshake. As Fate would have it, I did not see John again for the next quarter of a century, but he was a man I had the greatest regard and liking for : we had hit it off as partners pretty well, even if no luck had attended our steps on our search for gold. He is dead now : peace be to his ashes.

Gus and I struck up north through the San Luis Park and then out by Fort Garland to the lower country and so on to the Arkansas and the Fountain River and the Springs. There I had much to talk of with many friends. I made Gus a gift of Jinks and my precious mare and he lost no time in getting a cow-punching job, not a hard thing to do at that time of year with cattle booming. Having arranged my business affairs satisfactorily, I lit out on the cars for Boston, where were more friends to say good-bye to and where I was lucky enough to find that I could save a trifle by taking passage on a steamer running direct to London instead of to Liverpool as the Cunard and all the swell steamship lines did. The result was that early in the summer I found myself once more on my mother's door-step at Wimbledon, and rejoicing in the most loving of welcomes. Those who have adventured in the ends of the earth will realize what I felt.

Well, things might have been worse. True I had failed to make any money, either in the cattle business or in the search for gold. But I had saved my capital and I had preserved perfect health in the glorious climate of the Rocky Mountains. Should I ever try my luck out there again ? That was what I could not then say, for I was tempted to try it in various directions.

CHAPTER XV

G. T. T.

G. T. T.—gone to Texas! That was how people used to put it in the old days when a chap had about exhausted other people's patience, and received and accepted a strong hint to be off.

Well, here was I in the train along with Charley and Gus, bound for Texas from Colorado ; for myself I won't quite plead guilty to the exhausted patience charge, but Charley, I fear, might have. Let me tell how it all came about.

I had put in a year at home in the Old Country, without finding there any opening that tempted me. I still hankered for adventures out on the Ragged Edge, much as I found I loved the Old Country now that I was at home again. All the same, one or two things did surprise me a trifle. For example, I had returned to my mother's house at Wimbledon, a comfortable detached house at the end of Ridgway Place with a nice bit of garden and lawn. It was the middle of summer when I got there, and about then even England can be a little hot sometimes. And now it was hot, and sleeping indoors in a bed I could not help feeling it a bit stuffy after eight years of the open-air life. So one night, feeling it rather hard to sleep, I took my buffalo robe and a couple of railway rugs and stole out in the small hours on to the lawn and lay down there to sleep the sleep of the cowboy and prospector. Remember this was near half a century ago, before the days of FRESH AIR movements, &c. So I laid me down peacefully and slept, but ere long I was aroused by a shake from a not too gentle hand.

I opened my eyes, and lo! here was a big policeman standing over me. I fear he had taken me for some new sort of tramp.

" Now then," said he in a severe voice, " what are you doin' 'ere ? "

I sat up innocently in my rugs. Happily this was a country where no one carried or needed to carry a gun, not even a policeman. I explained to him my idea in lying out there as well as I could. At first he seemed incredulous, but at last I succeeded in convincing him that far from being a tramp I was really and truly the son of the house.

" Well, sir," he said as my novel idea dawned on him, " you to be sleeping out of doors this way ! You'd ought to know better than that. You ree'ly ought ! "

Humbly I gathered up my rugs and the buffalo robe and went indoors again.

So this was dear Old England ! Is it to be wondered at that part of me turned to the Rocky

Mountains again ? Also, very badly did I wan1 to make a bit of money, if only it were possible, for I had hopes of being able to get married in case I could fix things up right. And of course to me in those days the chances of the Rocky Mountain country, for making a bit of money quick, appealed vividly. True, I had not done the trick in my previous eight years of trying, but the luck might turn, who could tell ? So leaving Old England I set off for Colorado again in the summer of 1878, and out there I met once more many of my old friends in Colorado Springs.

But Colorado, besides old friends, had something new to offer. The thing that was on every man's tongue there was the big boom up at Leadville. Leadville was a new mining camp in the old California Gulch up near Granite on the Upper Arkansas River. I had been there when I was with Matthews in 1869. On that occasion I went to look at California Gulch, because I was told that a few years earlier, in fact in the days of Pike's Peak or bust, there had been 3,000 men washing gold out of the gravel in the gulch ; but ere long all the pay-gravel had been worked out, and so, when I went to look at the gulch, those three thousand gold-miners had all moved on, and there were instead about three families living in the valley and just simply doing a little farming.

Since that date, however, some one had gone and found a rich ore of silver—I think they called it carbonates—in the deserted gulch, and since

1869 Colorado mining men had learnt a lot more about how to deal with refractory ores, and now 10,000 men, so it was said, were hard at work taking out the ore, while 10,000 more were trying to locate fresh discoveries of the same carbonates all over the mountain country for fifty miles around. Nothing attracts one so much as a good boom, and away I went to Leadville to have another look at what I had known as California Gulch. I went up with Jim Head, a son of Sir Francis Head, whom I had known in England. He was taking to Leadville a wagon-load of bottled beer from the brewery in Old Town, as Colorado City was called ; the new town, Colorado Springs, was dry. Jim had a team and wagon, and along with him, driving another team, went Oswald Petre, a son of Lord Petre, who, I think, had known Head before, out in the Argentine. Anyway I fixed it up to put my blankets on Head's wagon and go up with him through the Ute Pass and across South Park, camping out along the road. It quite felt to me like old times.

Petre had a span of first-rate mules and a good new wagon packed with bottled beer he also meant to sell in Leadville. The only defect about the wagon was that the brake needed fixing by a blacksmith in order to make it powerful enough for a rocky mountain road. But Petre judged that there was hardly time to get this done before starting.

" It won't make any odds, though," said he

M

cheerfully. " They're a real good span of mules, and I can make them hold back down the hills."

Petre was right enough there; he did make them hold back, if it was heavy on the team, and they obeyed splendidly.

However, at last, on the third day out we saw before us a pitch off the brow of a mesa that looked ominously steep. The road ran straight down it, and was not more than a couple of hundred yards long, but it did seem like the roof of a house, while to make matters worse the whole slope was covered with great lava boulders, one narrow strip only having been cleared for the road. At the sight of the pitch Jim got down to lock his hind wheels. " Better lock your wheels, Petre," he shouted, but that hero had already started down. He hated to take the trouble of getting out. The day was bitter cold, and he had tucked himself down snug and warm in the front of the wagon—his favourite position—with a thick pair of blankets drawn over him, and only his head showing. Jim and I stood at the top to watch how he fared.

Petre had the reins in his firm grasp, and that staunch pair of mules hung right back against the pole for all they were worth. For fifty yards they held the load, and then the weight began to overpower them; faster they went, and faster, till the next moment they had to gallop to keep the loaded wagon from smashing right into them. Unable to hold it they swerved leftwards off the road, and ran out among the boulders. Bang, bump, crash, jump, went the wheels over the rocks ; the wagon rocked like a small boat in a steamer's wash ; we saw Petre's head jumping up and down with the bumps like a jack-in-the-box, and we looked every instant to see the wheels fly into flinders and the whole outfit be smashed into matchwood. But, no. The stout oak and hickory of that wagon endured the shocks, and in a moment more we saw the mules come to a halt at the bottom, the wagon still right side up.

Then with our hind wheels fast locked, Jim and I slipped safely down and found that Petre had actually condescended to get out, and was looking at the mules' legs. They were cut and bleeding from the rocks, but no serious damage was done.

"Good old mules ! " said Petre admiringly. " If I sell them in Leadville I shall ask an extra hundred dollars for them, and guarantee them equal to the worst kind of mountain work."

" How about that beer ? " remarked Jim sarcastically. " I don't suppose you've got a bottle left unbroken."

We looked inside ; one of the cases had partly given way, and the sawdust showed. Petre fished out a bottle intact.

" Good old brewery ! " cried Petre. He knocked the neck off the bottle and drank it down. " Here's to the men who packed the stuff. I'll bet there aren't three bottles broken in the lot."

No more there were, as we found when he came to unload. We loaded with bullion as return freight, and travelled the same road back. The bullion from the smelters consisted of heavy pigs of lead with only some two or three per cent of silver in it. The owners took good care not to refine it till they got it safely out of the mountains.

On the way down, of course, we met strings of loaded teams coming up with supplies. The heavy freighting over the Leadville road was done by trains of a dozen or more four- or eight-mule teams. These big trains naturally were apt to carry things with a high hand, and single teams generally gave them the road. But Petre was a man who hated to give way to anybody, and had no particular objection to a row. He had carefully inserted about a pound and a-half of shot into the stout handle of the blacksnake whip, which in his hand became an uncommonly formidable weapon.

And so it happened that in South Park we saw a lordly procession of big teams descending a hill to meet us at a bridge over one of the forks of the Platte. Petre was driving in front and Jim and I behind. We looked to see Petre draw to one side and let the big train cross the bridge first. Not he. Tucked away snugly, as usual, with only his head showing above the body of the wagon, he drove his mules on to the bridge just as the leaders of the foremost team swung on to it from the other side, and the two pairs of mules stopped head to head. Of course the whole long wagon train was brought to an abrupt halt, and we heard high words passing between the front teamster and Petre.

Jim shouted to Petre to let them pass first, and at last very sulkily Petre reined back his mules and left the bridge clear. The teamster drove across, and, flushed with his apparent victory, he pulled up abreast of Petre's waggon, and looking scornfully down from his high box-seat, addressed a few personal remarks to the miserable little blank blanked one-horse outfit that had the cheek to try and take the road from their betters. When Petre was coiled down in his favourite position with only his head showing, he looked as small as anybody else, but he had not lost his voice, and that teamster received such an answer that he could hardly believe his ears.

"Dad burn ye," exclaimed the astonished driver of four mules, "shut yer mouth before I whale ye one across the face. The cheek of ye!"

And then Jim and I beheld a swift reversal of the parts. Inch by inch the gigantic form of Petre emerged from his nest in the blankets, as he straightened himself up to his full six feet two, a fiendish smile on his lips, and his strong right hand drawn back to smite his foe with that heavily-loaded whip. So fierce he glared, so huge he towered, that as he rose the other man sank, cowering lower and lower, till, unable to drop from his perch, he stretched out appealing hands to beg for mercy.

"Don't, mister," he cried piteously, "don't strike. I apologize. I'll take it all back. Dad burn me if I had the leastest notion you was a quarter of the size."

Petre seized him with his left hand and shook him like a rat, still brandishing the uplifted black-snake butt over his head.

"You—dodrotted—cowardly—skunk," he exclaimed, emphasizing each word with a shake of his victim. "It would serve you well right if I bashed your teeth down your lying throat. Next time you want to play road hog you'll perhaps look first and see who it is you propose to bully." He gave him a final shake and turned him loose. "Drive on now, and get out of my road."

Pale with fright, the man drove on, and the rest of the wagon train followed him, Petre, his fighting blood up, standing huge and grim in his wagon and watching each driver as he passed. Not a word came from a single man of them; such a meek lot of teamsters never was seen. And then Petre snuggled down again into his blanket nest, and we crossed the bridge and drove peacefully on our way for Bear City.

"There's a certain amount of moral force about Petre," laughed Jim.

To go back to my own affairs, at Leadville I roamed around and made inquiries. I had lots of offers to go shares in more or less promising silver mines, but the more I looked at it the less I liked it. Mining for silver, or even prospecting for it, was a game of which I knew absolutely nothing ; I would prospect for gold ; I was positive of that, but silver raised me out. If I had known any expert whom I could have relied on to advise me, I might have tried investing ; men, those who were lucky that is, were just now making their millions in Leadville—but to go at it on my own account meant risking the bit of capital I still possessed.

One thing, however, did catch my fancy up there, and that was horses. The 10,000 men looking for more carbonates all over the mountains had to have horses to ride, or at any rate to carry their packs, and that summer almost any sort of a horse or mule was fetching $100 or upwards in Leadville. Well, I had never been to Texas, but I had often heard Texas men say that you could buy all the horses you wanted down there for $10 a head. Buy at $10 and sell at $100. That seemed good enough to me.

True, Texas was about 999 long miles (or more) away from Leadville, and a good many of those long miles led through a country of outlaws and of possible Indians, to say nothing of the crossing of the terrible Llano Estacado or Staked Plain where there was no water for 100, or for 200 miles, according to where you made the crossing.

But I thought I knew a thing or two about horses, and as for driving a good big band of them and herding them at night along the trail, that would simply be like driving a herd of Texas cattle, as I had so often done ; then as to Indians and outlaws or "bad men," had not I already had some experience of them, both in Colorado and New Mexico ? In short, the net result was that I made up my mind to go down to Texas, buy a herd of horses, and of mules too, perhaps, and drive them up to Leadville to sell at 1,000 per cent profit ! ! !

Of course I was far too late for the current year, for 1878 that is to say ; so much time had passed while I was looking around that it was already autumn, and late autumn too, before I fixed up to go. But that was all right. I would winter in Texas, and spend the time there buying the horses, and then start up with them in the spring. I had heard unkind things said about the Texas climate as well as about its inhabitants ; for instance, there was the story of the man who, when asked about the climate, said: " If I owned Texas and hell, I'd sell Texas and live in hell ! " But I put that down to mere spite.

In the matter of climate there was really something to be said on both sides. Texas really could be very hot in summer and Colorado 50° below zero in winter.

Before starting I took my pony out to a friend's ranch (in a snow storm) to leave him and get my blankets and portmanteau. In the morning it was Charlie Wilson who drove me down to the Railroad Crossing, to take the train back to town. Unluckily the ranch clock was wrong, and the snowdrifts deep, and we missed the train, so there was nothing for it but for me to shoulder my traps and tramp to the Section House for shelter till a freight should come along. So I did, and of course found on my way that in consequence of the storm no freight had got through for twenty-four hours, and that one might come along any minute. I got permission to come inside and warm. The place was tenanted by a crowd of Irish navvies, and they told me the train would not stop till I signalled it. All right! I kept my eyes on the curve of the track through the window, and after a couple of hours' patience, the train come in sight. I gathered up my traps, dashed out and waved my hat and expected them to stop. Stop! Not a bit of it! Imagine if you can my disgust at seeing the last car disappear round the next curve, leaving me forlorn in the howling storm. Very forlorn indeed I returned to my friendly navvies. " You didn't half do it, man," said the boss. " When you want to stop a train you must get on the track right before them and spread your arms out and wave your hat like mad, and don't leave off till you see them shut off steam and put on the brakes."

I can imagine a more cheerful thing than spending the rest of that day watching through the window for the next chance. It might come any minute, and one could not see more than two hundred yards, and often not that, on account of the whirling snow. All day I watched till night came, and I began to think I should have to wait till the morrow, when in a moment round the curve flashed a bright headlight. Out I ran into the darkness, waving a cap in one hand and a lighted pipe in the other, hoping it would do for a lantern. Would they stop ? Yes—no—yes, by Jove, it was all right, and in half a minute more I was piling my traps into the caboose, and as they started again swung myself up, and off we went.

A few days later I was on the train, leaving snowbound Colorado and even more snowbound Kansas along with Gus and Charley.

I have not properly introduced Charley yet. He was an English boy, barely twenty, I suppose, but he was old enough to have acquired one or two awkward habits. His friends at home had tired of him and shipped him off to other friends in Colorado, and now these last friends had shunted him on to me. Charley was a cheerful youth, and not half a bad sort if you could only keep him clear of the drink and of evil companions ; he was none too strong in the head, like Tommy Dodd. I fancy that the American psychological experts would have classed him with the half-morons. But he had rather taken to me ; chaps like that sometimes did, and the end of it was that to relieve his tired friends (and I don't wonder they felt tired) I agreed to take him along, they, of course, paying for his ticket.

We all three slept well enough on the car, and woke to find snowbound Kansas left far behind ;

now we travelled under a bright if rather wintry sun, which shone on us all the way through the Indian Territory and so southwards ever into Texas. The sun was much higher in the sky than any winter sun I had ever seen, and it felt warmer down here, sure. Up in Colorado we had left every man wearing the very thickest and warmest woollen clothes he could buy. Here people seemed to have on cotton garments, and none too heavy at that. But back in Colorado every man almost was ruddy and healthy looking. Here were many pale-faced people, and I suddenly remembered the horrid name of fever and ague. But this was not the season for that scourge, and till summer came one would be safe.

I was interested in observing the various sorts of Texas people at the depots getting on and off the cars, and sometimes I got into conversation with them. The Texans one saw in Colorado were practically all cattlemen ; here they were of varying types both in mind and body. Some showed themselves to be a trifle inclined to be stand-offish, at least to an unknown man like myself coming down from the North, and then I remembered that it was only thirteen years since the war between North and South. But the real novelty to me was the coloured folk. Texas had been a slave state, and I had never been in one before. There never had been slaves in the Territories such as Colorado and New Mexico, and, except perhaps for a few coloured waiters in the town hotels, you never saw any people with negro blood. Here on the contrary, they were very much in evidence on the platforms in the shape of porters, hack-drivers, and so forth. It seemed as if a great deal of the manual labour down here was done by blacks; they were of all shades, from jet-black negroes to light octoroons hardly darker than Whites, but it was obvious that between the two races, the White and the Coloured, there was a great gulf fixed. It is not easy to describe exactly, but there the gulf was, and both sides apparently accepted it as part of the order of nature (as indeed it is) and did not seem to resent the fact. I had read about it before, but this was my first actual contact, and it was curious to reflect that up to thirteen years ago all these dark-skinned people had been slaves born and bred.

I had gone into another car away from Charley and Gus, and here at last I forgathered with an old-time Texan who was not in the least stand-offish but quite ready to converse amicably with a total stranger. I very briefly explained to him what I had been doing in Colorado, and how I came to be now on the cars.

" And a darned good notion too it was of yours, sir," was his comment. " You're coming to the right spot. Texas is God's country as sure as you're born ! "

I made a gesture of assent, but there did flash across my memory that gentleman who had remarked that if he owned Texas and hell, etc., etc.

"Texas is all right for Mexicans?" I inquired. I knew Gus had been there before, but I wanted all the light I could get on the matter.

"Why, sure," said the Texan, "that is so long as they behave themselves and don't start in to make trouble. Then, of course, they've got to be taught not to, taught rather sharply." The grin with which he said this was somewhat unamiable, and I thought it as well to explain my own position.

"I got along with them pretty well in New Mexico," I ventured.

"Oh, New Mexico, yes," he returned. "They've learned their manners there, same as here. It's over in Old Mexico there's some as has a grudge agin' Americans generally, and what's more they're a trifle too willin' to show it sometimes."

I pricked up my ears. Gus was from Old Mexico. "What makes them like that?" I asked.

"Oh, jes' the memory of old times," he said. "Mebbe you don't know the history of this part of the country?" he added.

"Not very well," said I truthfully enough. "I've heard some things though."

"Ah," said he, and paused. "Did you never hear 'Remember the Alamo,' eh?"

"No," I said, "I can't say that I have."

"Crockett? Bowie? Travis?" he went on. "Never heard of them?"

"Oh, yes," I said, recovering myself, "I believe I did. Crockett was a grand frontiersman, wasn't he? And it was Bowie who invented the knife, I think? Weren't they killed in Texas long ago?"

"Sure," he answered, his eyes gleaming and fixed on mine.

"Tell me about it," I said. "I'd like to know more."

"Right you are," he said, still fixing me with his glance, "but it was before you was born, I reckon, long before."

I looked to be in my twenties.

"It happened more 'n forty years back," he went on. "You see a good many Americans had moved into Texas, which was a part of Mexico in them days. And they kind of got tired of Mexican Government. It was supposed to be a Republic, but all that meant was that the man who could cut most throats came out on top and called himself President, and then all the world had to kowtow to him."

"It reminds me," said I, "of what a New Mexican once said to me about the wild Indians. El Capitan de los Indios es aquel que ha matado mas hombres. The Captain of the Indians is he who has killed most men. The chief who has taken most scalps of course he meant," I added.

The Texan grinned at me again. "I can see you've bin thar, right enough," he said, "and you've got hold of their lingo too. Wal', as I was sayin', we 'uns in Texas got tired of Mexican Government and set up another Republic of our own, quite independent. We hoisted the Lone Star flag and ran our new Republic of Texas to the Rio Grande.

"And then the Mexicans got up on their ear and started to invade us. Ther' was a good many thousands of 'em too," he added, "and I guess we didn't hardly have one man to their ten, all told. So the Mexicans crossed the Rio Grande and invaded us and marched straight on San Antone. The Alamo was the strong place there, and Crockett, Bowie and Travis was in it with 130 men more. That was all against them thousands. The Mexicans took the Alamo by storm, and every last one of the Americans in it died fighting. Every last one of 'em. There's a saying goes like this : ' Thermopylæ had her messenger of death. The Alamo had none.' Now you begin to understand, eh ? "

" Yes," said I, " I've heard of ' Spartan Leonidas and his brave hundreds three.' I'm ready to believe the Alamo was your Thermopylæ."

" Ah, but there was Goliad too, and that wasn't no Thermopylæ. Fannin and four hundred Texans were there and knew it wasn't any use to fight the whole Mexican army, so they made terms and surrendered. Henry Clay said afterwards in the Senate that the terms would have been respected by a horde of Kalmuck Tartars. But the Mexicans just disarmed their prisoners and then took them out in batches and shot them. And President Sam Houston couldn't do nothing. The Mexicans just drove his handful of Texans back and back till he was up against the borders of the United States, and there he'd got to stop. Santa Ana was in a strong position on a sort of island and Sam and his men were bound to attack."

" Did they swim ? " I asked, feeling nothing was too wild for this story.

My friend hesitated, then he looked at me with a dry grin. " Sam wasn't taking no chances," he said. " It was ' root little hog or die ' that time. They crossed to the island by a wooden bridge, and then Sam sent back a couple of scouts to chop it down behind them, and told his men there wasn't no going back and the butchers of the Alamo and the Goliad was in front. So the Texans just went in shouting, ' Remember the Alamo ! ' took the guns and wiped out the Mexicans. Santa Ana got away but they captured him next day."

" Did they skin him alive ? " said I.

" Sam knew a trick worth two of that," grinned my friend. " He just kept him wrapped in cotton in his own tent and sent him back to Mexico labelled ' with care '—as soon as he'd made him sign a treaty giving the Lone Star State complete independence. Of course Santa repudiated this treaty as soon as he was safe home, but that made no difference. A bit later I was one of them the song tells of :

'At the age of sixteen years I joined the Ranger Band
We went from San Antonio down to the Rio Grande!'

and we kept them beyond the Rio Grande for ten years, and then the United States had to take hold. The Mexicans were fools enough to make war on them, and so they just waded in and taught them a lesson—good! Took California and the whole country across to the Pacific along with Texas, New Mexico and Arizona and Colorado where you've been——"

"Yes," said I, "I know that much. I've heard men in Colorado say, 'Git a plenty while you're gitting!"

"That's precisely what they done. But for all that you understand we haven't forgotten the Alamo and Goliad nohow."

"No," I admitted, "it takes a good while to forget such things."

"And it ain't always a wise thing to forget too mighty quick," he commented. "However civil we behave to Mexicans we keep our eyes peeled."

And I decided I might do worse than keep my eyes peeled when it was a question of Texan v. Mexican.

CHAPTER XVI

BENTON'S PASTURE

AT San Antonio it did not take me long to buy a wagon and a span of mules and light out into the country. The town had temptations for Charley that I wanted to avoid, and indeed for Gus as well, too. We wandered westward over towards the Rio Grande. The country was mostly undulating like the Plains, but it was not so bare. Much of it was covered with mesquite brush, a low-growing tree not very unlike an acacia and provided with terrible thorns. The grass was unlike the Plains too, it was not the short curly buffalo grass I had got to know so well, but a larger and stronger sort, not so very unlike a glorified buffalo grass, and this was called mesquite grass. Like the grass on the Plains, it was nature-cured and so gave good feed for horses and stock all winter. Nor were there any frightful blizzards down here ; no storms like our Colorado " zephyrs," as with sardonic humour we used to call them. Snow was practically unknown. If a Texan wanted to describe anything of a dazzling whiteness, he did not say as white as snow, but as white as cotton. However, there wasn't any cotton being grown in the part of the country we were in : the cotton-growing section then was down along the Gulf of Mexico, but I have no idea whether it has spread by now to other parts.

This western part of Texas was almost as little settled up as the Plains. Wire fencing was just beginning to come in, but most of it was open range left free to all, and now I saw where the vast herds of long-horned cattle that we knew in Colorado had been and were still being bred. Horses there were, too, in great plenty, but they were of Spanish bronco stock, and as in Colorado, they ran in half-wild herds, and they fended for themselves summer and winter, and were only caught and handled and broken when they were three or four years old. I priced them very carefully and anxiously at the various ranches were we stopped, but the $10 broken horses of which I had dreamed from the stories of the Texan cowboys I had met were not easy to find. $15 and even $20 were the more usual prices. Still, even $15 would leave me a good profit if I could sell them in Leadville at $100, and my hopes ran high.

It was easy enough to lose your horses in this country of dense mesquite scrub, and it became obvious to me as soon as I had bought even a few that the question of holding them would soon be of paramount importance. Gus and Charley could drive a bunch all right, but they couldn't well night-herd them too, and besides, one wanted the stock to be free to feed at night and not to stand bunched with a man on guard. Obviously, the thing I needed, and needed badly, was a good safe pasture.

Luck favoured me. I ran across a young Scot, Benton by name, who had bought a large piece of land ; I think it was land owned by the Texas Government ; I don't remember if the U.S. had any public lands in the State. Texas having come into the Union as a full-blown republic, owned her own land, while that in the rest of the Territories taken from Mexico by the U.S. of course belonged to the conquerors.

Anyhow, Benton had a very fine piece of pasture-land, as big as the biggest sort of an English park, with wood, water and grass, all A1. He had by this time spent a lot of his money in putting a wire fence all round it, and hadn't quite enough left to buy cattle sufficient to stock it properly, as he proposed to do. Under the circumstances, it did not take us long to come to terms. I settled to pay him so much rent for permission to put my horses in the pasture till the spring came, when he hoped to be able to get some more cattle and feed the grass off himself.

So Benton's pasture became my head-quarters for the winter. We turned in the horses I had already bought, and Gus and I wandered far and wide picking up what horses we could at any reasonable price, while Charley kept camp. He rather reminded me of Tommy Dodd whom John Miller and I took along. It was quite safe to leave him there, so long as temptation was far away, and Benton's society was a good tonic for him.

Gradually I began to get together quite a lot of horses and mules, and then one day a Texas man arrived and cautiously inquired for me. His story was that his Boss had heard of me, and how I was buying horses, and he would like to see me on the matter.

Of course, I consulted Benton at once ; I always did so when I could, and I was a little taken aback by his reply.

" Well," he said judicially, " you might be all right with him, and then again you mightn't ; it's hard to say for certain. You see, the way he describes it, his Boss is living out somewhere between the Nueces and the Rio Grande. Now that's the outlaw's country. The Nueces is the dead-line for sheriffs."

Well, I knew the border was a rather lawless district, but I hadn't quite been aware of that fact. The Rio Grande of course was the line between Texas and Mexico. The Nueces River ran roughly parallel to the Rio Grande for a couple of hundred miles or so, at a distance of perhaps fifty miles or more, and then turning away from it more to the east fell into the Gulf of Mexico. I knew there were outlaws on the

border, but the Nueces the dead-line for sheriffs !
That sounded a pretty tall order.

All the same, this man who had come to see
me from across the Nueces seemed a very decent
sort of chap, and he assured me very confidently
that I could do a good trade with his Boss. I
felt the temptation ; I discussed the matter with
Gus, and once again with Benton ; and in the
end I rode off with my new friend down to the
Nueces, and across it, and out into the border
country. A bit anxious I felt, that I must admit,
but my guide seemed so much quite all right
that I kept my fears well out of sight.

I was alone with him, for I had left Gus with
Charley at the camp. Gus had offered to come
if I wanted him, but he clearly did not like it
at all ; Benton also told me that he would be
much safer in camp, as the outlaws were not on
very good terms with the Mexicans, and were
liable to resent it if I brought along a Mexican
and gave him a chance to see where they were
camped. So Gus was left behind.

Also I did not take my Winchester along. I
now carried a new-model ·45 Winchester, an
improvement on the old ·44. If I was going to
visit a band of outlaws this splendid A1 weapon
might tempt somebody's cupidity, while against
such odds, against such a crowd as I expected
to find, I knew no weapon would give me any
real chance. Of course, I wore my Colt, but
every one did that.

Also I wore "shaps" or chaparrejos, which were heavy leather leggings coming right to the top of the thighs, where they were held up by a belt. These were a necessary part of a horseman's armour in all that part of Texas against the cruel thorns of the mesquite.

My guide led me a long day's ride westwards through the mesquite scrub, following the trails made by cattle where the scrub was too thick for comfortable riding ; and at last towards sundown we came out on a beautifully well-grassed abra, or opening, where a lot of rather good-looking saddle-horses were feeding at ease, and some eight or ten well-armed frontiersmen sat or lay round a fire at which the cook was getting supper. One thing I noticed. They mostly wore two cartridge belts, one for rifle and one for revolver ammunition.

My guide introduced me to his boss, whom I will call Mr. Brown. He greeted me very cordially, advised me to hobble my horse—of course, I had unsaddled—and turn him loose to run with theirs, and invited me to supper. So I sat down and ate my grub with my new friends and enjoyed it thoroughly. They seemed a very pleasant lot, men of the same general type I had known so well when I was ranching in Colorado. They did not talk at all of the things they had done or give themselves away in any sort of manner. The cook fed us with plenty of excellent beef, but nobody made any remarks about that, and naturally I asked no awkward questions. It was none of my business, anyhow, where the beef came from, and I knew there were plenty of wild cattle in the scrub. But Benton's saying about the Nueces being the dead-line for sheriffs would keep cropping up in my mind, and I realized this was No-man's land.

Supper over, we lit our pipes, and the boss drew me a little on one side to talk. He had heard, he said, that I was buying horses and he wanted to learn more. Obviously, I had nothing to conceal, so I told him the simple fact that horses were fetching pretty good prices up in Colorado, and I had come on the cars to Texas to see if I could pick up a bunch of them down here cheap enough to leave a profit and drive them north over one of the great cattle trails.

"Quite a sound notion of yours, too, I reckon," said Mr. Brown, when he had heard me through. "And now may I ask," he went on, "how much might you be paying for horses?"

"Oh," I returned easily, "horses vary and prices vary. You know that better than I do. But on the average I find I can get useful horses for $10 or $12 a head." I put the figure as low as I could without absolutely deviating from the truth. What was the use of telling him that sometimes I had paid more for extra good ones.

"$10 to $12," said he meditatively. "Why, I reckon I could let you have horses cheaper than that."

"Could you?" I answered eagerly. "But that's just what I'm on the look out for. What price do you think you could say?"

"Wal'," he replied cautiously, "of course that rayther depends on how many you want. Is your herd about made up?"

"Oh, hardly," I said. "If I got them cheap enough I dare say I could do with a hundred more. But have you a hundred?"

"Mebbe I could lay my hands on a hundred for ye," he remarked tentatively. "But how much would you be willin' to give? That's the important question."

"You're right there," I answered, "but for me the question is rather how much would you take?"

Mr. Brown rubbed his chin meditatively and pondered the great question a moment. Then he said abruptly:

"I kin let you have a hundred horses at $5."

"That would suit me down to the ground," I replied, much pleased. "Yes, I'll take a hundred horses at $5. When could they be delivered?"

"Wal' now," he answered, "that's hardly a thing I could say right off. It might be in two weeks' time, or it might be a trifle more. P'raps you're not aiming to start out jes' right away?"

"Oh, a couple of weeks or even three would be all right," said I. "I don't reckon to pull out till the grass starts, and they tell me that's

liable not to be for a month yet." I paused.
"There's only one thing," I added, "that I've
got to stipulate for. By Texas law no herd can
leave the State until it has been inspected by the
State inspector, who verifies all the brands. I've
got the bills of sale for all my stock and the brands
set down. You see, I shall arrange for the State
inspector to come and have him certify my bills
of sale before I light out. That's quite clear,
isn't it ? "

Mr. Brown looked at me with a quizzical grin,
a look that I seemed to remember having encountered before. It seemed to imply that—
well, that despite my "shaps" and my Colt, I
looked a tenderfoot still.

"Ah," said he regretfully, "you're aiming
to show your herd to the inspector. But you
wouldn't get no bill of sale out of me. You'd
hev' to take them horses wet."

"Wet ? " I queried. "I'm afraid I don't quite
follow you. What's wet mean ? "

"Why, it means wet," he answered. "You'd
have to take 'em jes' as they come out of the
Rio Grande."

And then it all flashed on me at once. Mr.
Brown hadn't any horses to sell just yet. He
had not the slightest intention of parting with
the fifteen or twenty good horses his party had
grazing there in the abra. What he proposed to
do was that he and his men should cross the Rio
Grande into Old Mexico, lie around on the quiet

there for a few days not too far from the river, spot a good herd of Mexican horses, ride in and cut the herd, by night no doubt, run them to the Rio Grande and swim it and then deliver them to me in Texas. They certainly would be wet when they arrived.

Of course, this was No-man's-land, and this was the sort of way its inhabitants lived.

"I'm sorry," I said, with real regret. "I'd have liked a good bunch of $5 horses. But, as I've got to have that bill of sale with all the brands put in, I'm afraid it's no go."

How would he take it, I wondered. And here was I utterly in the power of these lawless men if they liked to hold me a prisoner for blackmail. And away over yonder—and how far it seemed—was the dead-line for sheriffs, the Rio Nueces.

But I had no need to feel unhappy.

"I'm darned sorry too," agreed Mr. Brown, "I'd hev' well liked to corral that $500, but as you say it's no go, wal', it can't be helped. Let's turn into our blankets, and to-morrer we'll show you the way out of the brush. Of course, you needn't mention to any one 'ceptin' Mr. Benton as you've seen us."

The outlaw was as good as his word. Two of his band did show me the way safely out of the brush next day as far as the Rio Nueces, and told me just how to strike from there to make Benton's pasture. We parted on the friendliest terms, and I have sometimes wondered if outlaws have always been as hard cases as they're painted. Perhaps, however, it was just as well for me that I only saw their best side.

But I do know that Benton was most unfeignedly relieved to see me safe back, and so, most emphatically, was Gus.

CHAPTER XVII

SPANISH MULES

WELL, the $5 horses were no go, but there were other chances of a bargain still left. Mules would sell even better than horses in Leadville, and I heard that farther to the south-west in Texas the Mexicans raised a good many. This was worth thinking of.

Americans used mules to an extent quite undreamed of in England. In the days before motors nearly all the heavy hauling in America was done by mules. They bred big mules sired by huge jackasses specially raised for the purpose, of the breed of Old Spain, not little Mexican burros. These were great hairy brutes, 14 to 15 hands high, and the dams were good American work-mares, a trifle bigger than the jacks.

The reasons for using mules are simple enough. Take a fifteen-hand mule and a fifteen-hand horse. The mule will pull two or three cwt. more than the horse. He needs only about three-quarters as much hay and corn. He is seldom sick or sorry except for an occasional colic. His hoofs are harder than the horse's and grow so slowly

that the shoes do not want resetting so often
The mule lives longer and in fact he is a more
economical animal in every way.

The one objection to him is that he doesn':
love you. He doesn't want to do what you want
He fears the whip, and you can make him pull a
load all day quite well or carry you on his back
all day at a fair pace, but he won't race for you
I never yet heard of a racing mule. He can do a
good gallop on his own account, but just for you
he won't. Stick your spurs into him and try to
make him head a wild cow : he will gallop for
you, but always a bit behind the cow, and he
keeps saying all the time, " I don't want to. I'd
rather not. I'd rather not, and what's more I
won't." Splendid for his endurance on the trail
and for carrying a pack, he's no sort of use at a
round-up as a cut-out animal. But that don't
matter when you can get lots of horses who love
the cutting-out game, and will gallop themselves
to death for you, if you ask them. Brother mule
takes another view of things altogether.

So as my negotiations with the outlaws had
come to naught, I thought I would try among
the Mexican ranchers for mules, and with this
object I struck out south-west along with Charley
and Gus.

It was the upper part of the Rio Nueces which
was called the dead-line for sheriffs, as indeed it
well might be if, as Benton had told me, there
were 3,000 men wanted by the sheriffs between

it and the Rio Grande. But towards the Gulf of Mexico it ran through a settled country, and down there the Rio Nueces was the true boundary line between the Spanish and the English speaking inhabitants of Texas. One could not help being amused at the decided way in which their mutual distrust was expressed in the form of gratuitous advice given to strangers. "Bound for San Diego, are you?" remarked a Texan at a ranch where we "nooned" on the Oakville road. "Do you think the Greasers will let you get there with that fancy span of mules? I'll tell you what it is. You'd better trade 'em off for a pair of the 'ornariest' Spanish ponies you can find, and then mebbe you'll get through. You don't want to take nothing worth stealing into that country. Lemme trade you for 'em."

I disregarded this disinterested advice, but we did take great pains in choosing our camps and certainly did not find his fears verified. The other side of the shield was presented to us when we got to San Diego.

"Risk of losing your stock about here? Oh, dear, no, senores," said the emigrant gentleman from Old Spain who kept the store where I stopped to buy bread and corn. "Bad people there are in truth, but they are intimidated here—they dare not touch you. But how did you escape the robbers in Live Oak country? Those ruffians do but live off the plunder they get from unfortunate wayfarers and on the cattle they steal from us. They enter even into the river to rob."

The river, of course, was the Rio Grande. I thought of my friend Mr. Brown and his offer of horses " wet."

Truly a cheerful account of the Americans of the frontier did our Spanish friend entertain us with : the worst point about them, according to him, being that the biggest rogues were always either in office themselves or else in league with the officials.

Before reaching San Diego we heard of the fine Spanish mules bred by a family named Perez who owned a large grant of land on which they had 4,000 or 5,000 head of horses and raised the best mules in the country. Besides this it was told me that they were men of a good stamp— upright and honourable—in whose camps one would be safe, which was more than could per- haps be said of every rancher. As my object was to procure a herd of mules, and to do so with- out having to pick them up in small lots, but if possible to get them all from one man, I deter- mined to try them. Of course in true Mexican style these ranchers or large landowners did not live with their families out on the ranch as Ameri- cans would have done. They made their homes in the little country town of San Diego, whence the owners sallied out at intervals to look after the peons who took charge of the stock. After a short search we found old Don Pablo Perez, the head of the clan, at the house of one of his sons. Picture to yourself a grey-bearded man with the features of a Spaniard but the complexion much darker, erect as a lance in spite of his 65 years, with a commanding voice and a piercing eye that gave him somewhat of the air of an old army officer. It being a bitter cold day he was wrapped in a blanket of course, in true Mexican style, but he wore it with a dignity that really made it more impressive than any king's robes. Well, he asked us in to dinner, and I told Charley, who had never seen Mexican customs yet, " Now you are going to see how high toned Mexicans live."

He ushered us in, and making a low bow said, " Aqui esta su casa,—here is your house." I could not help thinking that the proffered house (it belonged to his son) was not very much to boast of, for it only had three rooms and I do think I have seen better in the much-maligned cottages of the English agricultural labourer. Clearly the family of Perez, though he had the grand manner, was not nearly so high socially as that of Capeza de Vaca in New Mexico. Here in San Diego, for instance, the kitchen had no stove or fireplace, but one end of it had a stone or adobe bench four feet high built across it, and on this the fire was made, the smoke going up an enormous chimney built over the bench. In keeping with this the sleeping arrangements were as primitive as you might expect. The beds

o

were made on the floor, but during the day they were rolled up against the wall, forming a sort of divan round part of the room, and served as seats.

We sat down in the room next the kitchen to wait for dinner, catching glimpses through the open door of the womenfolk engaged in preparing it and of a whole herd of barefooted imps who we rather fancied had several fingers, none too clean, in the pie. The women, crouched on the earthen floor, were engaged in grinding maize (previously boiled) between two stones, from which it emerged in a sort of paste ; this was then flattened out with the hands into thin cakes and baked on an iron griddle.

Presently dinner was served and I saw Charley begin to look rather blue. We were ravenously hungry and what was put on the table was merely a couple of dishes, one containing beans and the other a suspicious-looking mess, which turned . out to be composed of much the same materials as a Scotch haggis, along with a pile of maize cakes, tortillas as they are called ; also we were given a saucer apiece. No coffee, no bread, no cups, knives or forks. The mode of eating was simple. You helped yourself to beans or haggis in a saucer and used a piece of tortilla to scoop it out of the saucer into your mouth. Don Pablo kept calling out to the women in the kitchen, who ate by themselves and not with the men : " Ah, how savoury this haggis is ! What sweet meat ! " with the tone of a man who felt that his praise was worth something.

When the meal was finished a small girl brought in a jug of water and a glass, which was handed round and we all returned thanks to the donor of the feast—"Gratias por la comida, Don Pablo " —and retired to the shelter of our wagon to appease our hunger on bread and molasses.

We began to fear that Don Pablo's herd might prove as unsatisfactory as his dinner, but we were agreeably disappointed.

We came out to his ranch according to agreement, saw some of the stock, and I made a satisfactory " trade." He then departed on some business of his own to the Rio Grande and left his four sons to make the delivery. I hired temporary pasture near here and proceeded to receive the mules.

The corral was about 100 feet in diameter, with a smaller one opening off it. Early in the morning, as soon as breakfast was eaten, the vaqueros drove a mañada, or band of mares, into the corral. The mañada included a number of young stock and a few grown-up mules. Garcia and I went in and looked at them and decided which would do, not a very easy matter, as they were very shy and ran round so that it was hard to get a good look at them. The mañada numbered from 20 to 100 head, and we seldom could find more than two or three mules in one that suited us, and when all these animals were running about it was not so easy to decide. However, we would point out one, and at once two or three vaqueros were after him with their lassos. It is not so easy as one would imagine, from what one reads about throwing the lasso in books, to catch one particular head among a crowd all bobbing up and down. Soon enough, though, the noose would fly over the head of the victim, and then, such bounds and plunges as you see! The man who had caught him threw his whole weight on the rope, ploughing up the ground with his feet as the animal jerked him round the yard ; two or three more men ran to his assistance and a regular tug of war began. Others ran round with their lassos and tried to catch the unlucky animal by the fore or hind feet, or else to urge it towards the little corral. The mule bounded forward—the lassos were thrown at the feet and missed, the men who had hold of the rope braced themselves as it tightened and the mule swung round with a jerk. Pulling, hauling, swinging this way and that, they dragged him at last to the little corral. As he jumped through the gate, a quick hand flung the rope round his fore-legs and jerked them from under him and he came flat on his side to the ground with a thump that you might hear a rifle-shot away. In an instant somebody was on his head, the shears were brought and his mane and tail clipped, and the hot brand pressed for a moment on his shoulder. Then the ropes were taken off, he was released, jumped to his legs and joined the others which had already undergone the operation in the little corral.

I wish some man who can draw men in action and give a real sense of ease, strength and skill to his figures, could see this thing and make some sketches. I have never watched anything so quick, so lively and so various. No two animals act in exactly the same way when roped. It is not so monotonous as our athletic games are apt to be. Sometimes a rope is not well thrown and the noose, instead of being jerked tight just as it settles over the head, is allowed to fall as far back as the shoulders. Then the mule has the advantage and you can see him walk off dragging a whole string of men across the corral. Sometimes an unlucky throw catches two heads in one noose, and then, such a struggle as the pair make, trying to get free from each other !

As fast as we got one branded Garcia and I went into the corral again and picked out another and then the scene was repeated. As soon as we had got through a mañada the gate was opened and they were allowed to rush out. Outside was a mounted vaquero in waiting who turned them whichever way was desired and they disappeared. In a few minutes appeared more vaqueros with another band. We all crouched down inside so that the animals might not see us; the timid mares came up, wheeled and dashed away, were headed and brought back and again urged on up to the gate ; then one bounded inside and the rest rushed in after her. Finally the gate was closed, we stepped forward, examined the band, selected our mules and again the vaqueros tried the tug of war.

So well organized were the arrangements of the Perez men that one mañada was hardly out of the corral before another was in, and so in two days they managed to run through some forty mañadas, out of which we got between sixty and seventy mules, as many as I desired to have, as I reckoned that was about the number we could break between Texas and Colorado. Next, the problem was to get them to the pasture I had hired from Benton.

You see every mule is fond of the mares in the band in which he runs. The mule is a childish creature and never seems to be quite grown up. It is wonderfully fond of its mother and its aunts long after it is quite old enough to take care of itself, and as soon as it is separated from them it sets up a dismal cry that exceeds in volume and sonorousness anything I ever heard from any four-footed creature. If it gets loose its first idea is to run as fast as it can to the spot where the mañada is wont to range and hunt for it until found. So our mules, if turned loose, would have run forty different ways at once and have scattered over 100 square miles in an hour.

This would not do at all, so we had to keep them in till all were finished, and the third morning saw about twenty of us strung for half a mile from the corral gate on our eager ponies waiting for a race.

First of all the vaqueros brought up a mañada of three-year-old fillies, all bays; how pretty they looked! These had no foals and they were to run with the mules and help to steady them. They brought these young mares because they did not want a mañada with little colts in it for fear they might get hurt.

The mañada of mares was driven into the corral and mixed with the mules, and the whole lot "milled" round and round by a man on horseback to get them well mixed up and warm for the run. Outside you could see the horses of the vaqueros prancing and tossing their heads; they knew very well that there was a chase on hand and got as excited as so many race-horses at the starting post. At last the gate was opened and out they poured on the gallop, mules in the lead of course, with their heads away up in the air and beginning to sniff and whinny for their lost mammas. No time was to be lost now. Before they could begin to scatter, the vaqueros were behind and on each side of them, shouting and halloaing and waving their coats (the coat was taken off and waved in the hand to frighten the mules). Away they went up the flat as hard as they could tear, up the hill, down the other side, and across the arroyo and through the brush. I and one or two more who were less experienced galloped in the rear of the band, two or three of the best vaqueros were in front and the rest on the flanks. Well the men knew the country and how to steer them, avoiding the worst places and the thickest of the brush. Through the dust and the forest of ears in front of me I dimly discerned the uplifted hands and waving coats of the vaqueros ahead and understood how they were pushing the terrified herd first one way and then the other, though where we were going or what kind of ground it was I did not know in the least. One could not but get a little scratched by the mesquite thorns at first (in spite of one's shaps) but after running against one bough one took care to dodge the rest. The natives, of course, all had their chapparejos to protect themselves.

After the first couple of miles the pace began to slacken, and before we had gone four miles the panting herd, dripping with sweat, were glad enough to stop and take breath, as indeed were our horses. We dismounted to slacken and then tighten our cinches, and after a few minutes started again, this time in a walk, the men in front keeping the leaders back. The mares had had more than enough of it, and as soon as the herd strung out a little fell into the rear, while most of the mules were in the lead. Two of the vaqueros, taking advantage of this, dashed in between, and at one stroke we had most of them separated. A few minutes we held them, while as quietly as possible the few mules left with the mares were cut out and put with their fellows in front ; similarly half a dozen mares that were ahead were cut back to their companions. Presently we had the mules all by themselves, the mares were sent off in the charge of a vaquero back to their range, and we started the mules again in a gallop. The ground was smoother here and the pace even faster than before ; in three miles or so they were glad to come to a standstill again at the temporary pasture I had arranged for.

Here we said good-bye to the crowd, who lit their cigarettes, politely wished us success with our stock, and said, "That's all right," to our proffered thanks, and rode off home.

Garcia had made arrangements for me with two Mexican vaqueros, men from Old Mexico like himself, to help us drive the mules from there, and in the end we got them all safe to Benton's. We turned them into the pasture, and I went and fetched up the bell-mares, as well as the band of gentle horses I had already bought. Ere long the mules accustomed themselves to their new companions and gradually quieted down. Nevertheless, we herded them all day at first and watched them at night in the corral to be on the safe side. In the end the mules accepted the change and fell in love as deeply with their new set of mares as they had been before with the previous ones. For such is the nature of a mule.

CHAPTER XVIII

ON THE TRAIL

A T last the time had come for me to start with the herd of horses and mules, on the long trail to New Mexico first and so on to Colorado. But before anything else I had to get the herd inspected, and I arranged with the peripatetic official who ran that part of the State business to come, as I had so carefully explained to Mr. Brown, and do the job.

He came, and proved to be a very pleasant gentleman, but alas, his fees were not small! He gave me no more trouble than he could help; he just looked casually at those bills of sale with the brands entered on them which I had been so particular to provide myself with; took a good look at the horses and mules which were duly coralled for his benefit; declared that he could see the brands on them were all right!!! and passed the whole lot. I think he stamped officially all my bills of sale, took the cheque which I wrote for him, and—vanished.

I believe I could have got those $5 "wet" horses passed right enough, but all things considered I was glad I hadn't tried it.

Now there was nothing to detain us any longer and I said good-bye to Benton and started on my slow journey of 1,500 miles up through Western Texas and over to the Pecos Valley, which had to be followed the whole length of its long course through New Mexico, and then on across the Raton Mountains into Colorado.

I had eight Mexicans hired to drive the herd and the wagon and to do the cooking. With Gus, Charley and myself, the party numbered eleven. The last party who had gone through had numbered thirty.

I had a certain amount of knowledge of what I was up against. Benton had warned me that there were no sheriffs beyond the Nueces, but there were far worse dangers.

What I feared in the first place was a stampede, and, secondly, the waterless drive across the dreaded Llanos Estacados or Staked Plains, a drive which to many has proved a veritable Jornada del Muerte, or Journey of Death. Last of all, I reckoned the danger from outlaws.

The men on the Texas ranches I passed always did swear that although there was no danger to be feared just around where they lived, a little farther on I should have to be on the look out for a terrible gang. Finally the constant warnings against the terrible gang just ahead got to be quite a joke with the herders and me, for we never seemed to come up with it.

Then when we should get to Lincoln County

we knew there was a little private war going on there, in which hundreds of men had already fallen. It was a war between wealthy stockmen, who hired gangs of ruffians to fight for them, and these gentlemen shot down their rival ruffians from ambush whenever they got a chance ; and whenever they came across a man they didn't know they were apt to treat him as an enemy, especially if he had anything with him worth stealing. But I had lived two years in another part of New Mexico which was not exactly peaceful and had come out unscathed, though I had, alas, lost friends, and I was ready to take my chances of getting through now.

Altogether, the historian of the cowboy, Hough, had some ground for his verdict when he wrote "South-Eastern New Mexico was without doubt as dangerous a country as ever lay out of doors."

I knew also, and any U.S. troops I came across confirmed it, that there might be danger from roving bands of Indians, but I did not know that the leader of the strongest of these was Victoriano the Apache, who just at that time had broken away from the Indian reservation and was on the war-path, burning, massacring and looting all over the country I proposed to travel across. By luck—or the mercy of God—Victoriano and I missed each other, but now, forty years after, I ask myself, "Que diable faisais-je en cette galère ! "

We did take reasonable precautions. Often we drove off the trail at nightfall and made a fireless camp safe from enemies in the sheltering darkness; and I also decided, if necessary, to apply for an escort of U.S. troops. The frontier was being patrolled by two rival authorities: the Texas rangers who were white men employed by the State of Texas, and the regular U.S. cavalry who were mostly coloured men with white officers. The former had many of them been in the Southern Army, rebels, as they were called in the North; the latter were often negroes who had seen service on the other side in the Civil War. As may well be imagined, there was not much love lost between them. Still both parties—each acting on their own—did their best to keep in order those 3,000 outlaws and raiders.

As I said, I had decided to ask for an escort from some of these soldiers; but although the officers were more than civil, indeed friendly, they said they had not a man to spare, and, much as they regretted it, they could do nothing to help me.

As it would be too tedious to describe the whole four months or more of our journey over the trail, including a list of our hundred odd camping-places, I will try to give some idea of the job I had undertaken by telling of a few difficulties we met with. My plan was to strike the Pecos River near its mouth and follow it up into and through New Mexico. To get to it one had to make first for the head of the Nueces. Night-herding, of course, was necessary the whole way, and the night had three watches, la prima, la media, and la alba. We guessed the night hours by Las Guardias, as the Mexicans call the stars of the Little Bear, which acted for us as an hour hand revolving round the Pole.

One night I went on guard with Leonardo Gonzalez, a man from Old Mexico. He was small, but very strong, very plucky and a splendid rider. He and I took the morning watch, la alba, and the night was so warm that I just turned out of my blankets and did not even put on a coat. About half an hour later clouds began to come over from the east and distant thunder was heard.

Presently rain began to fall, and I put on my English waterproof which was strapped to my saddle, and hoped for better weather. But by three o'clock the rain was coming down in sheets, and it was as dark as pitch between the flashes of lightning which came every minute. Now Athanacio Sanchez and Gus appeared through the darkness ; Athanacio also hailed from Old Mexico, and was an A1 good man. We four placed ourselves in front of the herd, which with tails to the storm were steadily moving to leeward. How the water did splash down on our backs ! The ground was all a-swim, and between the almost incessant thunder-peals rose the hoarse chorus of the delighted frogs. Where they can all have been through the drought we had during the earlier part of the spring is a mystery, but now there were thousands about.

The effect of the lightning on the huge masses of leaden clouds that every flash revealed was grand in the extreme. It is wonderful how a little excitement and the momentary expectation of a stampede rouse one, and so add to the keenness with which one takes in a scene. Suddenly the wind dropped dead, then it whirled round to the west and blew right back again harder than ever. Then in a moment it seemed as if the sky opened ; there was a blinding flash and a deafening peal at the same instant. By the glare there was, as it were, photographed on the eye the picture of springing horses, bounding in every direction as if a bolt had fallen in their midst. Off they went, and in one moment they were past us, and it was up to us to head them. Away we flew, helter-skelter through the storm and darkness, shouting to the frightened herd the inarticulate cries by which one seeks to calm their fears. Presently we found ourselves at the top of a hill and once more at the head of the herd which we at last succeeded in stopping.

Gradually the heart of the storm moved away from us and the lightning showed itself more and more distant, until at last we were left quiet in the darkness with nothing to disturb us but the pouring rain. So we shivered till the grey dawn came on and then we returned to camp to get a bit of soaked bread and, best of all, a steaming cup of hot coffee. One wonders what people did before coffee was invented. Most men on the frontier would rather give up their pipe in camp than their coffee. To go without it in the morning would give any of us a bad headache, indeed, I believe it was as necessary to us as the morning dram to a drunkard. Pedro, the cook, got our blessings for that cup. My bed, unluckily, had not been put under shelter as I doubled it up to keep the dew out when I got up, and everything was sopping wet ; the rest of the party were not much better off.

At noon the clouds suddenly lifted and cleared off and the hot sun came out again. What a warm feeling of personal gratitude one feels towards him after such a night. In a little while the leaves and the ground were dry, and all the bushes round camp were decorated with blankets and clothes fairly toasting in the warm rays. We basked awhile for an hour or two and ate a meal of bread, beans and bacon, that were not half water, with much satisfaction, and three o'clock saw us on the road again ready to make ten miles before nightfall.

The next night I feared a repetition of the storm, for just at sundown, looking to the east, there rose up the most wonderful cloud I ever saw. It was a great pile of cumulus in the form of a pillar that stood half-way up the sky, narrow and perpendicular, with a great cornice overhanging from the top. All the underside of the bosses of cloud of which it was built were tinged rose colour by the setting sun, while the parts

P

in shade were a dark purple. Out of the middle of it shot lightnings. It was impossible not to think instantly of the "pillar of cloud by day, and of fire by night." But the wind this time was kind to us, and though it lightened all night on the eastern horizon the clear weather stayed with us, and we had no stampede.

It was no long time after this that the country was dry again ; mostly I rode ahead of the herd, but if I did happen to ride behind I could not often see much on account of the dust the 800 hoofs kicked up. Thus it happened that a few days later I failed to catch sight of a couple, a man and a woman, who were trudging beside the trail till we came abreast of them. He was obviously a white man, and it did seem hardly decent for him to be tramping afoot in those wilds, where no one ever walked if he could beg, borrow, or steal a mount ; he certainly must have some strong reason to explain his being there. The woman was a negress, black as a coal, who showed her brilliant teeth in a wide smile as we passed her, standing so splendidly erect with her bundle poised on her head. The man had his blanket rolled in swag fashion so that it hung across one shoulder, but on the other he bore a long military rifle. Could that explain things ? For I recognized it at once as a United States army rifle, a thing not often seen in the hands of a civilian. The United States Government was not in the habit of selling regulation rifles, and to possess one you must either be a deserter yourself or have got hold of one from a deserter. What category did he come under ? The line he was taking led to the boundary of Mexico where the Santa Rosa mountains loomed up beyond the Rio Grande ; once over there a deserter would be safe. But this man looked fifty and the United States army didn't have men of fifty in the ranks. Then there was the negress ; how was I to explain her ? They made a queer, not to say a suspicious, pair as they stood in silence till our dust should settle before they followed in our wake.

My crew of Mexican vaqueros, who never had any love to waste on an American, obviously thought that this was one who wanted watching. "You look out, capitan," said Leonardo Gonzalez in Spanish ; " you mind he don't steal one of your horses to-night. I've seen that man before. He was one of the old-time Texans who fought against Santa Anna, and took this country away from my people ; and afterwards he managed two hundred slaves for Colonel Beebee at his plantation on the Brazos. But now since the war he's been poor." Leonardo's advice was mostly worth taking ; that evening we cooked supper early, and then after dark resumed our drive for an hour, when we turned abruptly off the trail for a mile to make a second camp without a fire. Which dodge is a neat way to puzzle possible horse-thieves. Yet when we returned to the trail again next day the first thing that caught our eyes was the track of our queer friends; they had passed us in the night.

"Better you see if you find out something from him," hinted Leonardo when we caught them up again.

Leonardo always preferred that I should do the talking to a Texan.

"Well," said I, riding up to the man and saluting him, "you've fairly headed us. You make better time afoot than we do on horse-back."

His steel-grey eyes snapped.

"Sure," he assented; "but you don't need to be told I'm not out here on a picnic."

His mouth shut like a steel trap, as if to cut off any further admissions, and the minute the herd had passed he started to march on again, the negress following like a dog in his wake. I reined back my horse alongside him, and, ignoring his silence, began to talk, telling him where I had bought the herd and where I was taking them, and, in short, all about myself and my affairs. One by one his suspicions were laid aside, his reserve began to thaw, and presently his own story came out.

Leonardo Gonzalez had been, as usual, quite right. This man—Davison I think he said that his name was—had fought as a boy in the victorious Texas army thirty odd years before, and he had been Colonel Beebee's overseer afterwards on the Brazos. But when the great Civil War between North and South ended in the emancipation of the slaves and the ruin of the Southern aristocracy—a ruin which included their overseers—Davison necessarily lost his job. Practically he had to drop into the ranks of the poor whites. In Western Texas, however, to be poor did not mean starvation. A cabin by the creek, with a few half-wild cattle and hogs running in the mesquite, where also there was plenty of game to hunt and wild fruits to gather, offered an easy living. But about Davison's way of living there was one unusual feature. The poor whites were mostly men, born in that class, who married white women belonging to it. In the days before the war they owned no negroes ; they were not exactly welcome around the rich plantations, and they had little to do with the slaves on them. But Davison, when he was an overseer, instead of marrying a white wife, had taken a coloured woman to live with him. There was nothing unusual about that ; a white man was supreme among slaves ; the peculiar thing in this case was that between him and his black mistress a bond had sprung up that time only strengthened. Others in his place wearied of their coloured mistresses and replaced them by fresh ones. Davison happened to be of a different temperament. Of course the idea of marriage never entered into his head ; legal marriage between black and white either before or after the war was in most or all of the Southern States alike impossible and unthinkable. Yet as he told his story, and I looked back into the glistening eyes of the black woman at his heels, it was impossible to doubt that the link between them was as strong as any legal sanction could have made it.

"And now," said he, "what do you guess brings us out here? It's more'n ten years since the war ended, and there's a lot of young upstarts growed up since that wants everything their own way. 'Build a barrier betwixt blacks and whites,' is what they cry. 'Stop all intercourse between the races.' It's just politics of course. Them that raises the cry don't believe it, nor do they act up to it. They run round after the coloured gals, like they've allus done; yes, and the very ones that talk tallest about building the barrier betwixt is the worst when it comes to secret carryings on with the coloured folk. But what they are doing is to make it hot for a man like me that has been living decently and quietly. These young whipper-snappers have started a new Ku-Klux-Klan, and ride by night, masked, round the country warning us to quit. Yes, sir, they've warned me, that fought for the Lone Star flag before they was born. And they took out a man—I'll not say his name—but a man living like me, over on Ellum Creek, and they tied him up to a tree and whipped him with hickory rods till he was most dead, just because he wouldn't turn adrift his woman that he'd had for years. And now they've notified me that I,

and Sue here too "—the steel-grey eyes flashed
fire—"are to be served the same! I ain't
afeared for myself. I've got a right good wepping
that I had off a darky soldier "—he patted the
bright barrel on his shoulder lovingly—"but a
rifle don't save your woman when a skulking
secret society watches till you're out of the way
and gets hold of her. Them sons of dogs whip
Sue! Not if I know it! I went straight off into
Uvalde; I have a friend there; and I deeded
what stock I've got running out to him, so he
can realize on 'em and send the cash after me
when he gets it. But Sue and I have hit the trail
for Mexico. Yes, me, that fought the Mexicans
and took Texas from 'em—I'm going across the
Rio Grande to live with 'em. I've never loved
the Mexicans; they've got their faults, and plenty
of 'em, Lord knows; but they won't take Sue out
and whip her, nor me neither. I fought to make
Texas free; it ain't free no longer, now that
these skunks run it, and I'm going some-
wheres else. Where I'm free is the country for
me!"

"Are they following you, do you suppose?"
I asked.

"I dunno," he said, with a savage glance to
our rear. "I'll make some of 'em sick if they
do. But likely they know better than to try it.
Still, they might."

"Look here," said I, "you put your pack on
the wagon and travel along with us as far as

our roads lie together. You'll be quite all right. My Mexicans are a good lot."

"Thank ye," said he, "but I've played a lone hand so far, and I propose to play it so to the end. But I thank ye kindly for yer offer all the same."

The last I saw of the strange pair, Davison walked ahead, his face towards the Rio Grande, and the black woman trudged sturdily behind. Beyond the river the amethyst-blue Sierra de Santa Rosa in Old Mexico cut the sky. The road in front of them was clear, and over yonder no lynchers would doom them to the lash. Who finds freedom finds his country.

The colour question is one I have no mind to discuss. It opens up endless arguments. I will only say I don't think it has been solved yet; theoretically you may give the black man the same rights as the white; if the Ku-Klux-Klan prevails he doesn't get them, and the white man does not get them either if law and order be rights he ought to have. But Hayti, where the black rules, is (I am told) pandemonium; and I have heard of other islands not very far from it where the blacks are in a majority and are not oppressed. There (I am told) the whites don't have a good time exactly, and many of them simply quit. That solution of the problem is no better than the other.

I give it up.

CHAPTER XIX

THE STAMPEDE

FOR a while we travelled on, sometimes striking a clear stream or a water-hole where we camped in comfort ; or a pasture near a lonely ranch where we could get some feed ; but often on the bare uplands, where there was neither grass nor water, the stock had to be watched closely lest they should break back to their old comfortable home in the south.

It was near the Pecos River that our worst piece of luck befell us. Some forty of our stock got away near Emigrant Crossing and we only recovered thirty of them with no small expense of time and labour. And the very day that the vaqueros were bringing back to the herd those they had found the herd stampeded again, this time on the west side of the river and all the work was to do again.

The first stampede I was not with the herd, having ridden a few miles ahead with one of the men, as was my custom, to look out for a good place to make camp, i.e. good grass and a chance to get the stock down to the water. We waited an hour or more for the herd to appear and, as it was long in coming into sight, we rode slowly back to meet it.

When we did find it, it was sadly shorn, for about a quarter of it, and those the fattest and best-looking horses, had disappeared. There was nothing for it but patience and industry and I took the herd back to Richie's Ranch, where we had camped on good grass, and sent the best men out after the missing stock. The second stampede I will try to describe, as I was there myself and saw it.

There were six of us in camp besides the cook, but one had crossed the river to try to run in four head we had heard of not far off. At night-fall he had not turned up so I said I would take his watch and accordingly went on guard with Charley at sundown. The others brought their blankets out, as our custom is, and slept close to their picketed horses near. Well, Charley and I were keeping the first night-watch, La Prima as it is called, when we heard a shot down at the ford. "That is a signal from Athanacio," we both said, "he has brought the horses and wants help to cross them over to this side." So we awoke two of the vanqueros and sent them down to help him. In about an hour, Athanacio and they came in together. It seems the foolish boys had gone right down to the ford without using any of the inarticulate language by which you express to a brute that you won't hurt him ; and of course the scary creatures had rushed off at once and disappeared once more in the night. Athanacio said he would take a white horse we had picketed, as it would be seen farthest at night, put the mare's-bell on him and let one of the boys lead him along. If he could find them again, he thought the lost stock might follow him, and so off they went.

Athanacio was one of the finest men I ever knew. To him hunger and thirst, heat and fatigue and want of sleep seemed to make no difference. Day and night he was always cheerful, and always on the alert, and whatever was to be done he was the first to move.

By this time it was nearly midnight, so Charley and I awoke the other two men and set them to watch. As soon as the morning star was up, that is about two, the lazy rascals woke us again and we resaddled and watched the Alva. I rather enjoyed night-herding when I was not too tired. It gave one a better time to think over old scenes than any other. The deep stillness of the night, broken only by the cropping sound of the horses feeding and the occasional whinny of a mule who has lost sight of the mare, the fresh cool air, so delicious after the burning sun by day, the perfect clearness of the starlight and the curious keenness of feeling produced by the contrast between the peace which prevails and wild scenes that one felt all the time were vaguely possible, that might occur at any moment, were wonderfully favourable to reflection. Night-herding is not hard work on quiet nights. One sits still in the saddle or stands by one's horse, bridle in hand, ready to jump on in a moment, waiting patiently for the only thing certain—the unforeseen—sometimes alone, sometimes talking quietly to one's companion.

Towards daybreak it grew very cold, for the early morning air is " nipping and eager " in these dry high climates, so we made a little fire to warm our hands, going off every few minutes round the herd to see that all was right. At last the grey light began to show faintly in the east and the stars grew pale.

So we woke the drowsy sleepers and sent them in to get breakfast. Soon one began to see farther and what was background began to show as foreground, the herd which was a confused assemblage of indistinct shapes took on form and colour. Presently up came the sun behind the hills and it was day.

We were just discussing what there would be for breakfast and longing for a cup of coffee, the universal stimulant in camp life, when we noticed some of the mules at one end of the herd chasing something. It was a little Mexican dog that had come down from a neighbouring hut, the occupant of which was already out hoeing his little corn-patch.

A mule from pure love of mischief will chase anything that will run, be it calf or colt, lamb or wolf. We went round them and turned them back, but ere long the mischievous pup was back again and got another chase, and we went again to turn the herd.

Back they came, but the monkey spirit was fully awake in them now, they were full of green grass and excited by the sharp air and such antics and capers as they cut you never saw! Such kicks and plunges, some standing on their heads and some on their tails, just from pure love of fun. Then you might see the wild grey horses throw up their heads and snort. There were—alas, there were!—fifteen of them, all half-brothers from one mañada, the prettiest band of Spanish horses I ever looked at, and where one went all went. With crests erect and pricked ears they looked at the prancing mules and the spirit of mischief entered into them too. Right about they wheeled and, with manes and tails streaming in the wind, off they went and the whole herd after them. It was seventy-five miles before they stopped.

A stampede is a pretty thing to look at and a man who could paint it and give the feeling of the thing, the spirit of it, would make a fine picture. But when you happen to be the owner, and it is your hardly-kept property that is running heaven knows where, the picturesque side drops out of sight. Some say, riches have wings—mine had legs—about six hundred of them, and rather too good to be profitable. Charley was well-mounted, I was on a colt that had hardly

ever run and was thin and weak ; one can't always
ride one's best horses and the best were out after
the strays. Athanacio had taught us that the
way to stop a stampede is not to chase them
directly, but to let them all go and just keep them
in sight. Then the weak and poor ones will soon
stop, and then those in front, and gradually the
leaders, will come down to a trot and stop too
We lost so many the first stampede because the
vaqueros ran right on to the herd and cut it in
pieces, and the wild ones in the lead, finding
themselves alone and galloping horses behind
them, never stopped running till they could go
no farther. We have stopped half a dozen
stampedes since the first one by doing as Athanacio
advised.

So Charley and I struck out towards the hills,
leaving the valley to the herd. But the camp was
in the valley and they ran by the camp, and out
of the camp shot a hot-headed boy on a strong
young horse as hard as he could send him, and in
a moment he had cut the herd, and there were
forty or fifty of the strongest alone in the lead.
We put on a spurt and, getting a short cut on
them, Charley actually headed them and turned
them to the north. They always want to run
south, as that is the direction of their home, and
the love of home is the strongest of that bundle
of instincts we call an animal. He headed them
north, all but one, the fastest and wildest of the
lot. " Shoot him ! " I yelled. I was fifty yards

behind, but he did not hear or did not like to, and they broke past again, and away like the wind. Then indeed it was all up. Two Mexicans of Richie's driving up the milking cows from the "Vega" or meadow, below, tried to stay them; but in vain, and soon the best of my herd was a flying cloud of dust in the desert. There was nothing to do but let them go, and follow at a steady dogged jog-trot, they must stop some time, and then try to bring them back. The old vaquero now appeared, loping after the vanishing cloud of dust, and I rode alone through the hills. watching the cloud as it turned this way and that, running like the smoke of a prairie fire. Out they went ten miles to the soldiers' camp at a spring in the hills and back to the Pecos again, where one thirsty brute jumped off the bank into the water and was drowned—at least so we supposed, for we found his body there—and then they took right down the river.

This Pecos river is a curious one. It has high clay banks, and for miles and miles no animal can get in, or, rather, if it gets in it cannot get out, but must drown. Charley I saw no more of for ten days. He went back to camp with some ten head that had dropped out and were overtaken. Thirty miles below I found Manuel, the boy who had cut the herd, with fourteen more that had given out. It was past noon then and my head felt as if it was splitting, for to go miles, hungry and thirsty under a burning sun, is too much.

I lay down for half an hour under the shade of a mesquite bush and decided to send him back with what he had and to follow the trail myself.

Lower down the trail struck out from the river again and here I found the old man, his horse nearly dead-beat, returning empty handed.

"Where are the horses?" I asked.

He waved his hand vaguely out to the plain and said:

"The last I saw of them, they were striking out for yonder mesa."

"Well, there's no water that way for thirty miles and we can't follow them on tired horses. They must come back to the Pecos for water, inside of twenty-four hours; let's follow the river down and to-morrow we will cut their trail."

"But I have nothing to eat and no blanket."

"Well, we can stand it one night, and to-morrow night we will make Torres Ranch."

So I turned him south again and we urged our weary horses down to the river. There was no watering place, but I got down and baled up water for them with my broad-brimmed Mexican straw hat. Half the water ran out every time and I began to think I was a Danaid, but the thirsty brutes were filled at last and on we went. Suddenly appeared a little cloud of dust; nearer, it was horsemen; nearer still, and how glad we were to see the U.S. army blue. It was a little squad of half a dozen darkies with their sergeant and a white man as guide, who had been out on a scout on the Staked Plains. Had they any rations? "Not much," they said, but they could give us something. So with them we camped. I like darkies theoretically, but they are a dirty lot, especially darkie soldiers in camp. A handful of biscuit-crumbs from one of their haversacks is not appetizing, but Spartan sauce was plenty and down it went. The guide gave us some strips of jerked beef and a cup of coffee, and I did bless him for it.

At daybreak we started on down the river, having still some strips of beef and some broken biscuit. Towards noon we rested the horses, having found no sign of the strays, and I let the old man sleep while I took my rifle and went afoot into the hills to try for a deer. I saw plenty of fresh sign, but no animals except two hares, which were too wild to let me get a shot. I followed them a long way, but it was no use. They could hide in the brush, and run every time I got near them, and a running hare is a hard shot with a rifle. It is curious to note what a savage feeling one gets when one is very hungry and one's game keeps just out of range.

At nightfall we had found no game and no tracks, so we camped by the river again, giving the horses water in our hats. Just as I was pulling off my saddle, I looked round and there was a tiny rabbit, quite fearless, within three yards of us, sitting with wide open eyes, wondering, no doubt, what we were. It would have been very

Q

poetical to have let him go—indeed, I rather think I can call to mind having done something of the sort in youthful days—but in middle-life one gets to take a more practical view of things, and he was remorselessly knocked over and eaten. I may as well tell that it was by chance the queerest shot I ever made, the rifle bullet went straight through the rabbit from end to end, clearing it out as clean as cook would have done, without touching the meat. Two hungry men don't take long to finish a small rabbit, and there was plenty of time to enjoy the glorious sunset we had. The western sky all transparent gold with purple bars across it and such a weird flush of colour on the tops of the mesas to the east.

There is one truth worth learning about the beauty of Nature, and that is, that if one is resolute to look for it one will surely find it ; and, at times when one least expects it and perhaps most wants it, it does come, as a real power strong enough to cause one to forget cold and hunger.

For twelve days I followed those diabolic mules and horses and at the end I did not get them all. Forty of those I valued most, for they were the strongest, vanished into space ; the rest we drove up to camp and started once more northwards.

CHAPTER XX

BILLY THE KID

I WAS camped for noon at Lovin's Bend, near where the town of Eddy now stands, on June 26, 1879, when I saw Billy the Kid. Some weeks before I had spent a little time near a friendly troop of U.S. cavalry, whose warnings of the dangers that lay before me grew more and more emphatic the less I seemed to heed them. There was a civilian there named Sandy who had a contract for supplying hay to this particular post. He had happened to take a liking for me, and heard me joking with the officers over their warnings. He was a silent, reserved man, but he got me out alone and he spoke out to me and said :

" Those army officers were giving you no fool-talk."

" Well," I said, " it can't be helped. I've bought my stock, and I've got to go on with them ; there's nothing else to do."

" Well," he said, meaningly, " you go ahead if you're so set on it. But there's a man named Beckford you might find it mighty convenient to know. He's a sort of a boss among some of the fighting men in Lincoln County. He's a bad man when he starts in, shot his own son-in-law once for not obeying him, but he's worth your making a friend of if you could do it. I could give you a letter to him."

I thankfully accepted the letter, and sure enough some days' journey farther on up the Pecos, I ran on to Mr. Beckford and presented my letter of introduction. It so happened that half my herd stampeded badly just there, and we had to spend a whole month gathering the runaways, some of whom ran ninety miles before they stopped.

Mr. Beckford was extremely kind to me, and helped me all he could, and he and I went many days in company and spent many nights camped together in the open. He was a tall, lean, hardfeatured man, with a curious tired expression in his eyes. He was tired, tired of being for ever on his guard. All the time I was with him I never saw his watchfulness relaxed for an instant. His mind and body were perpetually on the strain. But he liked to hear me talk, especially about England, when he found I came from there. The life of civilization was to him a most interesting mystery.

" You want to understand as how I haven't any prejudice agin high-toned fixins," he said to me one night as we lay in the dark on our blankets under the stars. He never would go into the light of a fire after night if he could help it for fear of a bullet from the darkness.

"No, sir. Them high-toned Eastern ducks talk of us men who live out on the ragged edge as barbarians and uncivilized. But it ain't our fault. We do what we can. Why, I've bought a piano for my darters, and I'll bet it's the first piano ever hit southern New Mexico. Cost me four hundred dollars, it did, and it come four hundred miles by wagon too."

He was quite pathetic in his earnestness over the redeeming virtues of the domestic piano. One could hardly tell him that elementary civilization demanded that one should refrain from shooting one's daughter's husband even more peremptorily than that one should give her a piano.

But, as I said, he and I became very friendly, and I grew to have a real regard for him. His virtues, which were genuine, were his own; his faults those of the lawless state of society round him.

"Look at here, mister," he said, when the time came for us to part. "I've kinder took to you, and it makes me sorry to think of the trouble that lays ahead of you. It's kinder peaceful close around here just now; I've seen to that myself, but you've got some powerful bad country to go through yet, higher up the Pecos. Now I like to see civilized men come out here. I want to encourage 'em. There was a young Englishman came out here and brought a 3,000-dollar library with him. That was real tony. And danged if one of these sneaking, low-down gangs of rustlers on t'other side didn't lay for him, and shoot him all full of holes. Yes, he died, and I call it a danged shame. They died too. Some of our side "—there was a grim smile as he said this—" got after 'em and killed every last solitary man of the gang that did it."

"Well," said I, holding out my hand to Beckford, "let's hope that there's better luck in store for me."

He pressed my hand warmly. "Stop," cried he. "One word before you go. Let me tell you about one special man you want to watch out for : they call him Billy the Kid. He's a bad boy from Bitter Creek, if there ever was one. He killed his first man when he was only fourteen. He's killed seventeen or eighteen since, and he ain't barely twenty. That's not counting Mexicans or Indians. I tell you there's dreadful murders been done in this war, and there's a power of dead men's bones laying around lonely water-holes in Lincoln County. I know what I'm talking of. And this 'yer Billy he's fought on both sides ; he's been with me and he's been agin me. And he's cruel, sure.

"Look at here. I can't let you go like this. I'm going to give you a letter to him. Have you paper and pencil handy ? 'Cos I'll write it right now."

I produced the paper and pencil from my pocket, and the hardy frontiersman, standing by his horse and using the saddle for a desk, scrawled an uncouth missive, which he handed to me, and which I bestowed in the pocket again along with the bills of sale of my horses and other needful documents.

And then we rolled out with the herd, and for long weeks travelled up the interminable Pecos valley. At the few scattered ranches we passed we heard more tales of outlaws, but we met none ; though at Seven Rivers we saw three men come out from a ranch, mount in haste, and dash away off towards the Staked Plains on our approach. I went to the ranch and found a wounded man there, but he professed not to know who they were, and I did not inquire too particularly. I still thought I should never meet these much-dreaded outlaws personally.

I was suddenly disillusioned. We were camped for noon in some brush on the Pecos, some-where about the latitude of Fort Stanton. Except myself and the cook, Andres, who had started his fire, all the men were out at the herd, which was grazing. Suddenly one of the Mexicans galloped in from the herd with a white face.

"Señor," he began, "the robbers have come. They have got the herd." Of course he spoke in Spanish.

"What's that ? " I cried, springing up. "Have they run them off ? But I heard no shots fired."

"No," he said. "They are there with them as

if they were the masters. We cannot resist them : they are terrible men and have terrible rifles." He turned and looked back. " Behold, now they come here ! "

My eyes followed his. Four men were approaching quietly in a jog trot. I looked to where my horse stood tied outside camp, remembering my Winchester hanging in its big holster under the off stirrup. Should I make a bolt to get it ? To seize the rifle would give me away ; and then they would have me on toast, for they were within easy range, in fact, they were already here in the edge of camp. I must try diplomacy.

" Good day, gentlemen," said I, trying to look pleasant. " Won't you get off and have some dinner ? "

They accepted gruffly enough, or one of them did so for the party, and they swung themselves from their saddles and came to the fire. They wore heavy leather " shaps " and the ordinary cowboy dress, but what struck me most was what the frightened Mexican had with truth called their terrible rifles. Besides their revolvers they carried Winchesters of the very newest and latest model, and they wore two belts apiece stuffed full of cartridges, and the biggest of them—the man who filled my eye most—carried not one but two rifles, a sixteen-shot Winchester for quick shooting, and a Sharp's ·45 calibre, the famous " buffalo gun " of the plains hunter, for long range work. He was a giant in form, with a strong, hard, cruel

face and the shifty eyes of a wolf. Never did I
see a more evil-looking man. The moment I saw
his face I knew the Mexican had made no mistake
—we had to do with " terrible men."

" Hurry up, Andres," said I. " These gentlemen will take dinner with us."

The wolf-faced giant glanced at his companions
and a kind of inarticulate growl came from his
lips, accompanied by a corresponding gesture.
If I had to interpret it, the question he seemed
to put to the others was this, " Is it safe for us
to eat in this camp ? " It seemed an odd sort
of question to put ; they could hardly be afraid
of us, and there was no sign of their being pursued
by troops or anybody else. But his growl had
such a strong German accent, and in addition his
words stuck so deep down in his throat, that I
could not be really positive of his meaning. Anyhow, whatever his objections were they were
overruled, and presently the gang sat down.

There was a kind of surly strength about these
men that might well give reason for alarm. It
was not so much absolute swagger as that they
had a coldly arrogant air of owning the whole
camp. They sat down to eat, but their rifles were
across their laps and close to their right hands.
And they placed themselves not side by side, but
facing one another, so that their restless eyes
could see behind each other's backs ; thus no
one approaching from any quarter could fail to be
observed.

However, they accepted my coffee and sugar and bacon and biscuit from the cook, but then there was a pause—they delayed to begin. I myself, of course, was helped last, and they waited till they saw that I was eating freely. This was not mere politeness, for assuredly these gentry were not polite, and after they had watched me make a fair start they suddenly fell to with a kind of savage voracity.

Instantly the secret meaning of that evil German's question flashed across me. Poison was what they feared. There might be death in the pot ! Heavens, what a vile lot they must be used to be living among to think that. And then I remembered how two prison warders had been strychnined in Texas by some disguised outlaws while I was there. The remembrance did not make me feel any greater love for my guests.

It was an uncomfortable and unsocial meal ; they spoke not at all to me, only amongst themselves, and that in mumbling monosyllables.

" Come on to the herd," said the evil-faced German to the others, rising as soon as he had finished. They also rose.

" You'd better come too," said the smallest of the four with a casual glance at me. He was one I had not paid much attention to so far. He was quite boyish looking, not more than twenty, perhaps, slight made and lithe and very quick in his movements, with a curiously aloof and restless eye like that of an untamed wild animal in a cage.

His eyes never were still an instant, but roved perpetually over his surroundings and occasionally met mine full for a fraction of a second, only to be instantly shifted. If I were to describe him as "foxy" it would come as near his expression as I can get.

His tone was less truculent than the giant's.

"Yes," said I, moving to my horse, "I'm going to the herd; the men on guard must come to dinner." And at this moment three of them rode up. Their silent lips and white faces showed vividly how they took the situation. I wondered if they had seen some more of the outlaws out at the herd. When we had mounted the strangers deliberately took their places so that I had one on each side of me and two behind; and the boyish one now riding beside me asked many questions, where had I bought the horses, where was I taking them, what were they worth, were there any fast race-horses among them, and so forth.

I answered all his questions civilly enough and with perfect frankness. I did not say anything about having met any outlaws along the trail, but I did happen casually to allude to the number of troops of U.S. cavalry which I had met pat-rolling along the Pecos, whose commanders knew all about me and my herd. I heard a growl of scorn and hatred from the surly giant behind that seemed to carry a fervid anathema on the whole U.S. army. The slight figure riding beside me turned and checked him in such a decided manner that it began to dawn on me that this insignificant boyish person was the real leader, and not the big German after all.

"What'll you take for the lot?" was his abrupt query after I had finished answering his string of inquiries, as we reined up in full view of the herd which the Mexicans on guard had allowed to scatter out and graze.

"They're not for sale," I answered. "As I just now explained to you, they're going to Leadville. It would not pay me to dispose of them here. Say they cost me $15 a head in Texas (I purposely put them pretty low, so as not to excite cupidity) they might fetch $25, perhaps, here, but I hope to realize $50 to $60 in the mines. Therefore, it is no object to me to sell any of them along the road."

"Twenty-five dollars a head!" said the boyish leader with a malicious grin. "You'll have to give me time on them of course. Don't you think you could say a trifle less?" He was like a cat over a mouse, and obviously enjoyed it.

As before, the talk of the leader was accompanied by a running accompaniment of growls and muttered remarks from the others, the German especially. This time I made out some words that sounded like: " Nothing but Greasers " —his filthy term for Mexicans—" shoot up the d——d lot." "Take the hull outfit." " 'Bout time for ye to quit yer fooling, Kid."

Kid! Kid! Kid! Of course! Thick-headed idiot I had been not to see! This was the man himself. The slight, boyish figure, the smooth face, quiet voice, everything pointed to the young ruffian Beckford had told me of. I hastened to scramble with my hand first in one pocket and then in the other for my papers. As I did so, out of the corner of my eye I saw the Kid's hand resting on his pistol. He was not going to let anyone get him through the pocket with a Derringer, not if he knew it.

"Mr. Beckford," I exclaimed, still fumbling, "whom I think you know?"—he nodded slightly—"My friend Mr. Beckford with whom I spent some days down the Pecos below Emigrant Crossing, he gave me a paper for you, that is if I'm not mistaken. May I take it you are the gentleman they call the Kid?"

Even while his hand still held the pistol butt, his foxy face relaxed into a humorous smile— you have seen a fox grin?

"Yes, I'm the Kid," he said. "Go on."

"I got to have a considerable regard for Mr. Beckford," continued I—"ah, here's the paper —and he told me that I was liable to meet you along the Pecos, and that I might find this introduction of service," and I passed him the letter.

He took it in his left hand and nodded slightly to the other men who sat silently, as always, on either side of me. Their hands were also on their pistols, or within an inch of them.

Billy the Kid took the letter in his two hands and with obvious difficulty tried to decipher its scrawl. He called the German to his aid. They reined their horses a trifle back, and muttered to each other as they read. The evil face of the giant German grew sourer than vinegar. But whatever his feelings might be it was clear that what Mr. William the Kid said went. The latter turned to me. If he was disappointed, he didn't show it.

"Seems as how Mr. Beckford's quite a friend of yours," he began quite affably. "Friend of mine too, so it's just as well," he paused, "just as well for all parties that there hasn't been any misunderstanding."

Billy was a humorist, and his smooth, mobile face and foxy eyes showed how he relished the sarcasm in this.

"Well, sir," he continued, after a little pause, eyeing his comrades as if their obvious disgust was rather an extra joke, "you don't seem to jump at my offer to take the herd—on credit?" —again that malicious grin—"so I'm afraid we can't trade, but I wish you luck. I hope you'll get 'em safe to Leadville and a good price for 'em when you get 'em there, and if you see anybody along the road as wants to interfere with you, just refer 'em to Billy the Kid." He turned to the others and his tone changed. "Come on, boys, we've wasted time enough here, and there's business elsewhere."

I never was so glad to see anything in my life as the cartridge-girdled backs of those four ruffians riding off.

But when a year or two later I heard how Billy met Pat Garrett at Pete Maxwell's in Bosque Grande, and how Pat was too quick for him and shot him through the heart, so that Billy, who had got his gun out, actually fired (and missed) when he was dead, I could not help one half sigh of regret, for Billy to me had been a mitigated ruffian.

CHAPTER XXI

THE END OF THE TRAIL

AFTER this agreeable interlude our journey became monotonous and commonplace. Happy are the people who have no history !

The men broke in various mules as they had time, but the routine would be dull telling.

Any curious sights had really come before the great stampede. For instance, I remember swimming in the river and the turtles stretching their long necks up in wonder till I fancied for a minute I had got into a crowd of snakes.

Then at one ranch I saw oxen ploughing with the plough-traces fastened to their horns. And once I caught sight of a lonely shepherd on the hill above us and rode up to see if he would sell us some mutton, for it was long since we had had fresh meat. The man, I found, came from Old Mexico. He was a queer-looking creature clad in rags and armed with a long staff. He herded like David with a sling and a stone : whenever he wanted to turn the sheep in any particular direction, instead of troubling himself to run round them he would sling stones beyond them, and the rattling turned the leaders in the direction he wished. He had no meat and no power to sell.

Just as I was leaving him, I saw a great tarantula on its travels and pointed it out to him. It was amusing to see the cat-like enjoyment that brightened the face of the " Pastor " as he began to tease it with the long stick which he carried for killing snakes, rolling it over on its back and preventing it from getting away. The spider turned to bay at once and a more venomous-looking creature than one of these great hairy insects, with legs as long as a quill-pen, is hard to conceive. One almost wonders how it came that the serpent and not the spider was taken for the personification of evil. There is a drawing in Doré's illustrations to the *Inferno* of a gigantic spider carrying off doomed souls, which is wonderfully effective in rendering the sense of pitiless cruelty which they leave on one.

We had another day's march across bare and desolate country and the glare was intense, so we were glad indeed to make our noonday halt at some glorious springs above San Filipe on the Rio Grande. How delicious was a drink of the cool limestone water after the putrid horse-ponds which supply most Texas ranches with the first necessary of life. When one strikes such a spring on a roasting hot day, one feels as if one would like to pass the rest of one's life stretched out in the dark shade of the live oaks, only getting up at intervals to plunge again into the cooling element.

But a few hours of it is enough for anybody, and one is just as keen to be off again and face the dry deserts as one was before to get out of them. Nor indeed was there much rest for me here, for as soon as I had got a bite to eat I had to start off to the San Filipe settlement, a collection of " jacals " or Mexican mud-hovels in a desolate sandy flat a couple of miles below the spring. There is an outpost here consisting of a few cavalry and a couple of field-guns as a sort of protection to the frontier. Any service more odious than being stationed at this most uninteresting spot can hardly be imagined.

As this was the last settlement we should strike for hundreds of miles, I got some corn for the wagon-mules and bidding adieu to civilization —such civilization !—returned to camp.

We passed through some very wild and romantic glens in crossing the Raton Mountains and at the head of one of them I had the rare pleasure of finding an English family of good position. It was so queer to get off one's pony, all rough and ragged and sun-burned and step into the draw-ing-room of an English lady, full of pictures and knick-knacks of all kinds with books and music lying about.

We had a stampede the next night on the top of the Raton Mountains, but the mesa had rocky walls and the stampeders pocketed themselves in a corner as neatly as a billiard ball, and we got them next morning without any trouble.

And so, far on in July, at the end of four months' hard work we camped for noon on a certain bluff I knew which overlooked Colorado Springs, which was then just precisely eight years old from its birth, and there at our feet it lay, spick and span, with Pike's Peak and his fourteen thousand feet of bare granite glowing red in the summer sun for a background.

The Mexicans stared with intense interest, not at Nature's marvel, the glorious mountain, but at what lay below, the work of men's hands, the first genuine American city they had ever beheld ; for the wild little frontier cities they had come to know out on the Texas border were in fact largely Mexican both in style and in population.

But Colorado Springs was another guess sort of place altogether. Emphatically " The Springs " was high toned. It had been founded by a company composed of highly enlightened people, largely from Philadelphia, and its ideals from birth were total prohibition and thorough education, together with the natural consequence of those grand ideals, the shekels.

Now my vaqueros, though, like nearly all Mexicans, they had never been educated and were unable to read or write, had nevertheless heard great stories of the very rich mines lately discovered in this fine country they had lost to the Americans, and of the bonanza kings who owned them. They weren't worrying about grand

R*

red granite peaks; their imaginations ran on millionaires and millionaires' palaces. Presently Athanacio Sanchez, a tall Sonoreño and perhaps the best roper I had, stood up, and, looking at me, he singled out a large building with long rows of tall windows in the middle of the town which seemed to dominate the rest. He pointed to it with outstretched finger.

"Now, señor," he said, "is that one of the houses of the *ricos*?"[1]

I knew "The Springs" well; in fact, I had chased Texas cows over the site of it before it ever was born or thought of.

"No," I answered, "that's not a house of one of the *ricos*; that's the *escuela publica*."[2]

"A school for the sons of the rich men?" he queried; the vaqueros, unthrifty wage-earners, living from hand to mouth, were infatuated with the idea of the overwhelming importance of wealth and its possessors. Doesn't the poet say, "It is the poor man's one insatiate wish to know what wealth is?" The Mexican peons have that wish as much as any.

"No," I returned, "or, as I should rather say, yes and no. The sons of the rich do go there, but the school is a public school; that means that it is for the sons—yes, and for the daughters, too—of *todo el mundo*, of all the world. Everybody in Colorado Springs can send his boys and girls to that school to be taught, and taught free.

[1] Rich men.   [2] Public school.

In America everywhere education is free and open for both sexes alike, and for rich and poor."

Perhaps I was pitching it a bit strong, but I believe that, broadly speaking, it was true then, and that it is true to-day.

Here cut in little Leonardo Gonsalez, who had been listening closely to my words, his keen, bright eyes all the while roving from one to another of the roofs of the town lying beneath us. Now he, too, pointed with outstretched finger, and indicated a long massive stone building, a bit to the right, not so high as the public school, but quite obviously a structure that had cost money.

" There," he cried ; " see that ! Isn't that a millionaire's house ? "

" Oh, no," I said. " You've got millionaires on the brain. That's another public institution ; that's Colorado College. Boys and girls who have done well at the public school and want to go on with their education can proceed there and take up more advanced work. It is free, like the other, and open both to men and women. The only qualification is that you've got to show that you've got sufficient elementary knowledge to be able to profit by the advanced teaching. But it's quite absolutely free. The town pays for the school, and the State pays for the college. That's all the difference."

The little Mexican hailing from Chihuahua

was a natural-born fighter. Before now I had heard him shout " Viva Porfirio Diaz ! " when he got excited in some argument with the others. He was intensely patriotic. Brave himself (I can testify to that), he was a believer in the war-like spirit of his countrymen. He looked long and very wistfully at those two fine buildings, the finest in the new town, which the keen American spirit of progress had so honourably devoted to education right from the start. Then he swung round and looked at me, dark fire flashing from his indignant eyes.

" Do you believe, sir," he burst out, " that if we had had schools and colleges like that for our officers the Americans would have conquered and taken this country from us ? "

Perhaps his view of education was narrow and warped ; it was not a liberal education that he wanted for Mexicans, but one that would give them officers competent to command in war. Nevertheless, a nation's first business is to keep itself in existence as a nation, and here accordingly it may be that little Leonardo from Chihuahua was not far out. Officers competent to command in war are a prime necessary ; Mexico lacked them terribly in her hour of need ; let us give thanks to Heaven that in our hour of need the schools and colleges of Britain have justified themselves.

And back once more in Colorado Springs, I tried to sell my herd. But I found the market was dull at that season and that it might have paid me better to have rushed the stock through on the cars in February or March. Yet I did feel a bit proud—and thankful—to have done what no one had ever done before without armed guard or escort. The American teamsters I found were a bit shy of my unbroken beasts, so I got a couple of wagons and started teaming to Leadville on my own account, to wont the stock to harness.

I camped in South Park at the head of the railway track from which all the freight for the mines is hauled. It was a beautiful place to camp, right under the snow range, which puzzled my Mexicans for a while. They could not believe the white patches were truly snow.

It was while teaming that I heard a story that I cannot take my Bible oath is true, but most folk believed it. At the Leadville road there must have been fully five thousand mule-skinners engaged in hauling supplies over the stretch between the end of the rail in South Park and the great new mining camp. Leadville had the biggest kind of a boom on ; day after day rival coaches raced each other in over the road, and they used to come charging along past our slower-moving freight teams, crowded as full as they could hold of tenderfeet, both male and female, from the Eastern States. Often and often have I seen these new-comers gaze wonderingly out of the coach windows at us teamsters, as they were whirled by, as if we were to them some new and strange kind of wild beast.

One day it chanced that my train of wagons had halted for noon in a narrow pass, and was so drawn up as partially to block the road ; and Billy Windy, the stock jester of the camp, recounted with delight a snatch of conversation that he swore he overheard as one of the coaches picked its way through us at a walk. We had dumped our bales of hay beside our wagons in order to feed them to the mules, and we were sitting amongst them eating our own usual fare of sow-belly and hot bread as the coach-load of tender-feet went by.

" Oh, ma," called out a little girl to another inside passenger, and pointing wonderingly to us, " Oh, ma, look. There are those mule-drivers eating bread. Why, I thought they ate hay, same as their mules."

" Hush, child," replied the lady addressed as " ma," speaking with the nasal twang of the regular down-easter, " what nonsense you talk ! Why, they're part human."

I think Billy Windy invented that story, but it went the round of the camps, and it certainly hit the exact note. Part human—that was exactly what the outdoor men of the Great Plains and the Rocky mountains seemed to those Eastern folk.

I found breaking and selling the stock was a slow and expensive business, so I decided to turn the rest of the herd over to the care of a friend who would sell them off gradually and to start myself for England.

I paid off my Mexicans and at the last I had to say Adios to my old companion Gus. I left him comparatively well-to-do, but although his courage and courtesy brought him friends wherever he went—one American called him " the king of the cowboys " and swore he ought to be king among the Mexicans—money never stayed with him. He had the virtues and the vices of mediæval times. In the fourteenth century he might truly have been a king among men ; in the nineteenth he was merely a cowboy out of a job.

After setting him on his feet a couple of times I decided to allow him a small annuity, and twenty-five years later I saw my old friend again. He had come in from his ranch to meet me at the little frontier town. There along the squalid pre-tentious street, came little old Gus, squatted on the low seat of his wagon behind his thin bronco, and in five minutes I had my bag on board and we were off. Poor old Gus ! He told me he was only sixty, but he looked ten years older, he was so grey and so slow in his gait. But he was neat and clean as ever, and it was from his face more than from his words that I guessed how melancholy an old age is his.

Alas, the shandrydan was a relic ! What had been its springs once were gone, and it now rested on solid wooden blocks ; the seat was hard, I cannot say how hard to me, softened by a quarter of a century's ease, and the back was so low and so knobby that one couldn't use it at all ! 'Twas already afternoon, and the daily duststorm was rising ; we struck out south along the raw unmade city street with its myriad wheel tracks cutting it into deep ruts and a fierce south wind blowing the maddening dust wreaths up into our faces.

" How far is it, Gus ? " I asked with a sinking heart.

" Only twenty miles," he answered, " we may get there by seven o'clock ! " And it was now just after two ! Four miles an hour, and to think that he and I used once to ride racing speed after cattle on the old Squirrel Creek ranch ! We passed out of the dusty town, and our road rose before us slowly over the interminable swells of endless downs ; at last I was once more on the Great Plains. Yes, I remembered them exactly—the dry, dry surface, the scanty tufted Buffalo Grass no higher than moss, the long sweeping curving outlines of the skyline, like the backs of racing greyhounds, as Meredith somewhere says, and the enormous sky vault above. What I had forgotten was that awful wind ; it shrieked around us, tearing at our hats, so that we had to hold them on with one hand, while with the other Gus drove, and I hung on to the little handrail of the seat to keep myself on board. Through the worst of the dust devils we had to shut our eyes and trust the thin bronco to steer herself. How our eyes smarted! And to think I came 5,000 miles for this! Lord, how my cousin John would have laughed! For John had scoffed and said to my wife, "You'll see him home again in just three and half weeks. One day on the prairie and one night on the bare ground will do it."

After this I put on a pair of motor-goggles that luckily had strayed into the pocket of my overcoat, and for four hours we pushed over those bare downs against that awful wind, till on the summit of the divide it seemed strong enough to blow the thin bronco down. Here and there were sparse herds of cattle grazing on the poor grass. There had been no *good* rain for four years, said Gus. But as we dropped lower and lower the wind grew less, and lo! we had reached the cedar brakes, and between the sandstone bluffs that walled in the cañon were pools of water; beautiful doves and quail flitted across the road, and prairie dogs barked at us from their hillocks; and so we emerged at last into the wide flat valley of the Animas River, rich with dark-green alfalfa meadows and pale cottonwood trees. Here was a big ranch with capital good buildings and a great "aermotor" whirring round to raise water for the irrigated lands. Here were well-fed horses in a paddock, and all looked rich and prosperous. On top of the house-roof was an upper chamber of wire gauze, doubtless to sleep in during the summer heats, but through the gauze I also detected gymnastic apparatus. "A rich English company owns this," said Gus, chiming in with my thoughts ; "they have a Scotchman and an Englishman to manage it." In place of this wild cowboy comes the practical business man from across the sea, who irrigates his lands by the most new-fashioned apparatus and keeps up his muscle in a private gymnasium !

But this oasis was not our destination. Across the broad sandy bed of the empty river—empty but for a long, rock-bottomed pool—we bumped, and so up and out through a wilderness of the ghostly white trunks of dead cottonwoods, and into Smith's Cañon, a side valley of the Las Animas, a mile up which lies Gus's ranch.

"Este es mi palacio," he said with a bitter smile as we come in sight of the humble cabin. "This is my palace. I am poor ; but you knew that before."

Yes, I knew it. All the way across I had done the talking (when talk has been possible), for he had been thinking, what will his old friend feel when he sees the poor hut that is all he can offer him.

"Well," I answered, "it will give us shelter, and what palace could do more ? " and in we went.

It was small and bare, but well swept and clean, and it had four rooms built of humble cottonwood logs plastered with mud. Behind the hut was the green line of cottonwood trees, and the yellow sandstone bluffs of the Animas; a few cattle dotted here and there showed up dark, the rest was all a sort of washed-out khaki colour. But, after all, Gus had what no palace can enjoy—the elastic invigorating air of the summit plateau of the American Continent, and as you breathe it you feel as if it could bring the dead to life.

And he was not an absolute hermit. Near by lived a decent Mexican family with whom he messed. As we rode up to their hut in front of the door sat an old, old man, so old as to be past work, and hardly able to notice us. He was entirely occupied with the baby; he said " vaca " (cow), and then from low down in his throat came the call that every vaquero, every cowboy, knows. The child listened admiringly. This was no cheap, common, nursery moo-cow imitation, it was the deep-drawn wailing note of the bereaved and milky mother to the life. Then he raised his deep-sunk, faded eyes to mine as Gus and I alighted, and said as he gently patted the little dark head beside him, " Será buen vaquero, no ? " (He will be a good cowboy, will he not ?) " Surely," I replied with a smile, and the old man smiled too. For he was recalling the days of his own lusty youth, when he rode like a centaur and swung the wide-looped lasso, and " tailed " and flung headlong the most stubborn of bulls. Never again would he do those feats himself, but it was his hope that this tiny child beside him should be as good a man as he. Alas, that hope was gone as past recovery as his youth, for the day of the cowboy is over. He came, he rode, and he conquered, and now the barbed-wire fence had swiftly made him an anachronism. Soon even those who remember that life would be gone. The old, old vaquero would soon slip into the grave on whose edge he tottered; Gus, worn out prematurely with the hardships of a life that had its pleasures too, was a cowboy no longer; the future is for the child who will know nothing of the perils and joys of his grandfather's youth. " Ya se acaba todo," said Gus; " the old times are gone." And me— I had come 5,000 miles to photograph cowboys and round-ups as I remembered them a quarter of a century ago, and behold ! cowboys and round-ups are no more.

The big neighbouring ranch owner proved to be a kind and generous friend, but Gus's was a sad and lonely old age. He was obstinate in his belief that if he could only get a few cattle together he might begin in a small way and be a cowboy once more. He would not believe the day of the cowboy was done and their wild life gone for ever. Now he, too, has gone. *Requiescat in pace.*

I have done. But I think I may tell here a little story of one thing that was said of me after I got home. I was nearly the youngest of eleven, and I had an elder brother who was the best of good fellows, but he could not quite get over the temptation of letting off a little bit of sarcasm at the expense of his junior. Somebody remarked

R. B. TOWNSHEND, 1922

of me that like other men who had been alone much in the wilderness I had a great capacity for keeping silence.

"Well," said he, " you may talk of Dick being silent, but get him on the Far West, and it's like turning on a tap ! "

I hope the readers of this book (if indeed there are any) will not think the tap has been turned on too hard.

I should like to wind up with this story that I can take my Bible oath to. It is of a little girl from the East, and it was at a quiet boarding house in Colorado Springs where I stayed just before starting for home. The folks there were Eastern people, mostly come out for their health. I did not see any particular point in holding forth to them, and held my tongue pretty much till near my last evening there. Then somebody happened to turn on the tap, and I gave them a few of my Far West experiences.

Suddenly a dear little girl there clasped her hands and looked at me with glowing eyes :

"Why," she cried, " you're a perfect hero ! "

It was dear of her. But nobody ever felt less of a hero than I did just then.

And so my mind was made up to chuck the Rocky Mountains finally and try Old England again. I made my way home, and I want to set down here emphatically that the end of an adventure is not the end of life and the best part of my life was yet to come.

I got a job as assistant master at Bath College, under a man I loved and admired, that fine scholar T. W. Dunn, and married. After five years at Bath we moved to a village in Worcestershire, and then in 1891 we settled in Oxford where good friends permitted me to become a member of Common Room in Wadham College. I wrote novels and articles, translated Tacitus' Agricola and Germania, and also did Fourth Maccabees for Dr. R. A. Charles's Clarendon Press Edition of the Apocrypha, played lawn tennis, acted as Treasurer to the University Golf Club, shot at Bisley, and used my old Western experience in teaching all boys who came how to lasso and handle a gun.

When the war broke out I, of course, joined the University Volunteers and went with a party of dons down to the range. A sergeant was going round finding out the new-comers' experiences, and coming to me he said, " Have you ever handled a rifle ? " A shout of delight and derision went up from my friends, and the sergeant was a bit offended till it was explained to him that I had had some experience. When he tumbled to it he said, " The best thing you can do is to take that lot off into the corner, and show them what to do." So that was the last time I went to the range. I made one in my own garden, and week-days and Sundays taught all comers to shoot with my air-guns, and very good shots I made of some of them. I had schoolboys, Oxf. & Bucks Light Infantry, " cook's son and duke's son," dons and cadets, till my health broke down in 1916 and ended the training. And now at the end I can say life has not been a disappointment, and there is a good deal of truth in the line :

"And for His chosen, pours His best wine last ! "